HISTORY OF THE BUNA CAMPAIGN

December 1, 1942 - January 25, 1943

Published by Books Express Publishing
Copyright © Books Express, 2011
ISBN 978-1-78039-908-9

Books Express publications are available from all good retail and online booksellers. For publishing proposals and direct ordering please contact us at: info@books-express.com

COMMAND AND GENERAL STAFF SCHOOL
OFFICE OF THE COMMANDANT
FORT LEAVENWORTH, KANSAS

5 July 1943

AIR MAIL

Lt Gen Robert L. Eichelberger
APO 301, c/o Postmaster
San Francisco, Calif

Dear Eich:

    Your report on the Buna Campaign with its accompanying note of 17 June is a windfall to me and to the School. I am sincere in this acknowledgment.

    From the SWPA we have had very little informational material of the proper command and staff level. Only last week did Willoughby, enroute to Washington, give us a comprehensive view of the situation obtaining in your theater.

    Therefore, with the above explanation and apology, you can appreciate how glad we are to get your report. In order that we may keep on the beam and be of some value to the field forces I must have your current operations to guide our instructors along lines incident to this War, not WW I. Particularly, could you have one of your staff keep in mind our needs and ultimately furnish us, from time to time, with interesting operational material -- field and administrative orders, staff reports, etc. from a corps or divisional level? Classified, I promise full security measures. With your help, I hope to overcome our informal deficiencies in connection with the peculiar conditions inherent in operations in your theater. In this global war, graduates must have balanced instruction and not limited to a particular theater.

    All of us send our very best wishes for your continued success. I envy you your job and would give all to be with you -- in any capacity.

                                    As ever

                                    KARL TRUESDELL
                                    Maj Gen, U S A
                                    Comdt

HEADQUARTERS I ARMY CORPS
OFFICE OF THE COMMANDING GENERAL

June 17, 1943.

Maj. General Karl Truesdell,
Command and General Staff School,
Fort Leavenworth, Kansas.

Dear Truesdell:

Copies of the attached report have gone in through official channels. It strikes me however that you might be interested in reading our report of the Buna Campaign.

Today I read with great pleasure an article in the May issue of the Military Review written by Major Rudolph telling some very interesting sidelights on the campaign. Naturally I cannot speak with any authority as only the Ground Forces can do that but we did put a whole lot of time and effort into this report while leaving out things that were too controversial. If you and your good men find it of interest I would be glad to know it.

Give my affectionate regards to the Shallenbergers and the Lyles and any other of my old friends you may see.

With warm regards,

Sincerely,

Eichelberger

FOREWORD

This report is an account of the participation of American troops in the Buna Campaign.

Historically, the campaign is important because it was the first victorious operation of American Army ground forces against the Japanese.

From a military standpoint, the campaign is important because it teaches lessons, the importance of which varies directly with the remaining number of jungle operations to be fought against the Japanese.

This report was written on our return to Australia after the campaign. The material incorporated was obtained from official records made on the field of battle and from subsequent personal interviews with authoritative individual participants.

Lastly, and most important of all, the purpose of this report is to aid those who fight under similar circumstances in the future. Its value may be judged by the Allied lives it saves. . . and the enemy it kills.

Robert L. Eichelberger
Lieutenant General

TABLE OF CONTENTS

FOREWORD

PAGE

I. PHYSICAL GEOGRAPHY:

    1. Central Papua.   1

    2. Buna Combat Zone.   2

II. GENERAL TACTICAL BACKGROUND:

    1. Early Japanese Movements in Southwest Pacific Area.   11

    2. Initial U. S. contact in Buna Area.   14

    3. Summary of Situation at End of November.   16

III. OPERATIONS:

    1. First Break-Through to the Sea
       December 1-5.   19

    2. Capture of Buna Village
       December 6-14.   23

    3. Capture of The Coccanut Grove, and Preparation on Warren Front
       December 15-17.   26

    4. Isolation of Buna Mission, and Attack on Warren Front
       December 18-29.   29

    5. Capture of Buna Mission
       December 30 - January 5.   36

    6. The Sanananda Operation
       January 6-22.   39

IV. ORDER OF BATTLE:

    1. Enemy.   42

    2. Allied.   45

V. APPENDIX:

    Annex #1   G-1 Report.   48

    Annex #2   G-2 Report.   54

TABLE OF CONTENTS (CONTD)   PAGE

    Annex #3 G-3 Report.   64
      Inclosure A Field Artillery Report.   74

    Annex #4 G-4 Report.   78
      Inclosure A Ordnance Report.   86
      Inclosure B Quartermaster Report.   90
      Inclosure C Engineer Report.   94
      Inclosure D Signal Report.   100
      Inclosure E Medical Report.   104

I PHYSICAL GEOGRAPHY

1. Central Papua.

The area of the Papuan Campaign, to the date of writing, is roughly that of Map "A".

Since all maps and charts of this area are incomplete, the following information is based on carefully authenticated reports from competent ground and aerial observers.

General.--The Owen Stanley Range is the central ridge line of the Papuan peninsula. This backbone-like barrier rises steeply from the southwest coast to recede more gently to the northeast coast. At best it is a jagged, precipitous obstacle, crossed only by rain-soaked, hazardous, jungle tracks.

Numerous mountainous spurs run northeast and southwest from the Range. Up to 6,000 feet above sea level a large percentage of the area is covered with rain forest, while above to the tree line, is moss forest.

The ranges go up to 10,000 feet with peaks over 13,000 feet.

Winding their way down from these mountains are numerous rivers. In their upper reaches they are clear, fast rapids over rocky beds, but as they near the coast they widen to become slow and muddy with low, forest covered banks. During the wet season it is normal for these rivers frequently to flood coastal areas several miles in width.

Lines of Communications.--The only possible way to move by land from one coast of Papua to the other is by native track or trail. Because of the mountains and mud, none of these tracks is usable by motor transportation. There are no railroads in Papua.

While the immediate concern of this report is the Buna Combat Zone on the northeastern Papuan coast, a geographical explanation of the Theater of Operations should be made.

The Base Section of the Communications Zone was located in Australia. The Advance Section was located in Port Moresby. From Port Moresby to the Combat Zone there were but two routes over which supplies in bulk could be moved: by sea around Milne Bay, where there was a sub-base, and by air transport over the Owen Stanleys. It should be further noted that when the Japanese were being pushed back across the Owen Stanleys to Buna, there were NO adequate port installations on the northeast coast of Papua and only one usable air field: that of Japanese held Buna. To assist the American troops in their flights to the north shore of New Guinea, hasty air strips were established at Pongani and near Mt. Sapia, while the strip at Wanigela was improved.

2. The Buna Combat Zone.

General.--The Buna Combat Zone was located on the low-lying, flat coastal plain stretching inland from Gona and Buna to the foothills of the Owen Stanley Range.

The area is covered with dense jungle, reeking swamps, and scattered patches of kunai grass. Before the campaign it was largely unexplored by white man except along a few native tracks and from the air.

Off shore are many uncharted reefs. The sea, however, is usually calm and fog at sea level is unknown.

On the coast, at exactly 8° 38' South and 148° 26' East, lies Buna, which is variously known as Buna Mission or Buna Government Station. Buna Village, a cluster of native huts, is one-half mile to the northwest.

Before the Japanese arrived in the latter part of July, 1942, the Government Station had three European-type houses and about 260 native huts. Three whites and about 120 natives constituted the combined population of the Government Station and Buna

Village.

The key to Buna's tactical importance lay one and one-quarter miles south of the Government Station in a large patch of kunai grass--the air field. It ran northwest by southeast, was 800 yards long and about 60 yards wide when the meager Allied garrison retreated from Buna in July. During the next two months the Japanese extended the strip to 1,300 yards by 90 yards. Further, they put in blast bays and constructed a new strip 570 yards long and 60 yards wide immediately southeast of the Old Strip. Enemy planes were sighted for the first time on this new strip September 19, 1942. However, it was later found that this new strip was a dummy strip and the planes on it were, of course, dummies.

The importance of building and defending these strips is more evident in the light of associated distances:

Port Moresby	102 air miles
Milne Bay	200 " "
Townsville	800 " "
Salamaua	147 " "
Lae	167 " "
Rabaul	400 " "
Faisi	525 " "

For the Japanese, Buna offered a base from which to raid nearby Allied installations, with fighter cover. For the Allies it could mean an air base unfettered by Port Moresby's weakness-- the hazards of the Owen Stanley Range and its erratic weather.

Weather.--The weather in the Buna area is far from good but even so is better from an air point of view than that over the Owen Stanley Range. In the Buna area the temperature varies from a winter minimum of 64° to a summer maximum of 96° F. The mean relative humidity ranges between 78 and 85 percent. Thus a one degree variation in temperature is felt keenly by Europeans in the area.

The mean annual rainfall (for the past 12 years) in the Buna area is 113 inches, with November, December and January being

Creek near Sinemi Village before a rain

... after a rain

the wettest months. For these three months there is rain on an average of 14 to 17 days per month. Some of these rains defy description such as the torrential downpour of January 11, 1943, when eight (8) inches were recorded.

During the wet season, which is from November to May, violent rain squalls or "Gubas" are frequent, though seldom lasting more than fifteen or twenty minutes. At times, gusts up to 40 miles per hour have been noted. Tropical cyclones or hurricanes are unknown. Between November and May the prevailing wind is the northwest monsoon while winds from the southeast may be expected during the remainder of the year.

Typical slit trench in Buna area after a rain

Soil.--The soil near the coast is a light, sandy loam while further inland there is a heavy loam. Since paved roads are unknown in this area, anything from an oozing, slippery layer of mud to impassable bogs are the order of the day for the handful of native tracks in the area.

Vegetation.--There is an unlimited supply of drinking water in the area and a tangled lush of vegetation. Ninety percent of the region is covered with a labyrinth of jungle and swamps. Remaining are patches of kunai grass. Patches of this grass range from a few square feet in size to several square miles. The grass has broad, sharp-edged blades and grows to a height of six to seven feet. After being burnt off, tough, heavy tussocks remain.

Kunai grass in Buna area

The jungle in the area is a bewildering tangle of vegetation including many poison plants of which, however, only two are particularly troublesome: a stinging plant with a furry leaf and the thorny trailers of the lawyer vine (Climbing Calamus).

There are no stands of trees in the jungle which are of a uniform species but rather a large variety in any given small area. The pandanus probably predominates. The trees in general are soft wood and have wide buttress flanges—some of great size.

The swamps in the area were of vast tactical importance during the Buna Campaign. They are mostly nipa and mangrove and varied in depth from inches to well over a soldier's head. They are a stinking jumble of twisted, slime-covered roots and muddy "soup".

Both the jungle and the swamps give complete cover from aerial reconnaissance. For ground troops, however, any sort of observation or orientation is tremendously difficult.

Typical front line position near Buna Village area.

The only food available in the area is from small, scattered native gardens which had been thoroughly stripped by the Japanese. The usual crops are taro, yams, sweet potatoes, sugar cane, papaya (pawpaw), bananas and breadfruit.

There are two principal coconut plantations in the combat area. Immediately around and to the east of the Government Station is one, and at Cape Endaiadere is another.

Natives and Wild Life.--The natives in the Combat Zone were at one time war-like and suspected of cannibalism. However, they are now considered largely missionized and loyal to the Allies. Any sort of bombing put fear in their hearts and, with rare exception, they were found worthless for patrolling.

Wild life in the area includes wild pigs, a few species of fowl, and a few wallabies. While poisonous snakes are reported as numerous, few were actually killed during the campaign. Likewise, few crocodiles were seen.

Health.--Throughout the whole of New Guinea, including the Buna Combat Zone, the mosquito is considered as formidable an enemy as the Japanese. Europeans in New Guinea before the war looked upon malaria as Americans in the United States consider the common cold. Medical reports of the Buna Campaign (see Appendix, Annex #4, Inclosure "E") do not disprove this observation. As a matter of fact, the north shore of Papua is one of the worst infected malarial areas in the world.

Beside the ravages of malaria, dengue fever is also a common malady, while deadly blackwater fever is less common.

Both bacillary and amoebic dysentery are an ever-present possibility, as are jungle ulcers. The smallest scratch or cut must be treated instantly or infection will set in.

Sand flies are common along the coast. They are small enough to penetrate the average mosquito net, and to scratch their bite is to invite jungle ulcers.

Leeches are fairly common but can be removed by a touch of a cigarette or burning match. Any break they have caused in the skin must be treated against infection.

Scrub typhus, carried primarily by the numerous chiggers (Thrombicula Akamushi) in the area and secondarily by fleas infected by contaminated Japanese, developed during the campaign. There is no known innoculation against this disease.

Ring worm, Dhobi itch, "athlete's foot" and hook worm are also medical problems in the area. While gonorrhea and granuloma are common among the natives, most native women were hidden in the interior during the campaign.

Strategical Influences.--The terrain factors influencing the strategy of the Buna Campaign were vital considerations. (A pictorial presentation of them will be found in Map "B").

The Japanese positions were roughly at (1) Gona, (2) along the Soputa-Sanananda track and (3) in a perimeter, based on the sea, with Buna Village its right flank and the coast just below Cape Endaiadere its left flank.

Leading to these positions were five somewhat dependable native tracks:

1. Jumbora to Gona.
2. Soputa to Sanananda.
3. Soputa to Buna Village.
4. Dobodura to the Buna air strips.
5. The Coastal track north through Cape Endaiadere.

Conspicuously missing were any means of lateral communications for the Allies. Further, the swamp and jungle between each of these five tracks were such that cutting lateral tracks was a practical impossibility with rare exception.

In the Gona-Sanananda area the Japanese placed their positions on the only dry ground available. In the Buna area they did even better:

Coconut plantation at Cape Endaiadere. Note enemy bunkers.

The Buna Positions

The Japanese terrain utilization between Buna Village and the coconut plantation at Cape Endaiadere was perfect. With the sea to their rear, they anchored their right flank on Buna Village where the unfordable Girua River and Entrance Creek enter the sea. Since the wet season was at hand, it could be expected that the river frequently would flood the Soputa - Buna Village track--the only track approaching the Japanese right.

From Buna Village the Japanese perimeter followed Entrance Creek inland to where the Soputa Track forks to Buna Village and the Government Gardens. From this point the perimeter reached east across the intervening swamp to the northeastern edge of the Old Strip, down the strip to turn east along the New Strip and extend through the coconut plantation to the sea.

Naturally, the strips gave the enemy fields of fire. Further, the impassable, jungled swamp between the Dobodura - Strips track and the Soputa - Buna Village track precluded lateral communications between Allied forces attacking the Japanese flanks. For the Americans it was a two day march from their left flank near Buna Village to their right flank below Cape Endaiadere. But, at the same time, the terrain _inside_ the Japanese perimeter was such that they could move reinforcements quickly to any threatened point by truck or marching.

Thus, the enemy's brilliant terrain utilization canalized all potential Allied attacks into four narrow fronts: (1) through the swamp in front of Buna Village, (2) against the fork, or so-called "Triangle", of the Soputa-Buna track, (3) across the narrow bridge between the strips, and (4) through the coconut plantation below Cape Endaiadere.

II GENERAL TACTICAL BACKGROUND

1. **Early Japanese movements in Southwest Pacific Area** (See Map "C").

Twenty-eight days after Pearl Harbor, the Japanese bombed Rabaul. Seventeen days later they dropped their first bombs on New Guinea--with Lae, Salamaua, and Bulolo as targets. Two days later, on January 23, 1942, they landed in force at Rabaul and soon dispersed the meager Australian garrison to the nearby mountains. Thus came the Japanese to the Solomon Sea area.

With Rabaul air strips ready for operations, Port Moresby was raided for the first time on February 3. Exactly one week later the Japanese landed at Gasmata, New Britain, half way between Rabaul and the northeastern coast of New Guinea. This was five days before Singapore fell, February 15.

On March 8, the Japanese staged large-scale landings at Lae and Salamaua. Two days later, they bombed Buna. Meanwhile, in the Netherland East Indies, the Battle for Java had virtually ended.

As the enemy moved down the Solomon chain on the eastern side of the Solomon Sea, Washington announced on March 17 the arrival of American troops in Australia. Simultaneously came news of the arrival of General Douglas MacArthur in Australia.

During April, the Japanese occupied Faisi in the Solomons and during the early part of May gathered in Tulagi and Guadalcanal. On May 6, Corregidor fell and the Battle of the Coral Sea started. Enemy convoys moving south--for Port Moresby as it was later disclosed--were intercepted and on the 11th were turned back.

During June, in the Solomon Sea area, the Japanese consolidated; while to the northeast, his naval forces were again defeated, this time at Midway.

On July 22, some twelve days after the enemy occupied Kiska, in the Aleutians, they landed in force at Gona, a few miles northwest of Buna on the Papuan coast. In a matter of hours they were in Buna and pushing southwest towards Port Moresby. By July 28 they were in contact with the Australians at Kokoda, high in the Owen Stanley Range which separates Buna from Port Moresby by 100 air miles.

Came August and in the Netherland East Indies, the Japanese were completing their occupation. In the Solomon Islands the U. S. Marines on the 7th landed at Tulagi, Florida and Guadalcanal to establish beach heads, the defense of which is now legend.

On August 26 the Japanese landed at Milne Bay, southeastern tip of Papua. But it was an ill-fated venture. After fanatically attacking the numerically superior Australian garrison the depleted Japanese force fell back. By September 8, it was believed that they had evacuated a part of their remaining troops and it was known that only a handful of starving stragglers were left to work their way up the Papuan coast to the Buna base.

However, from Buna in the Kokoda region the Japanese were faring better. (See Map "A"). More than 5000 pushed forward over the Owen Stanley Range by the Kokoda trail. The Australian garrison was in retreat. Day by day the Japanese drove toward Port Moresby. Despite the steep, cragged mountain tracks, the rain-soaked, fever-breeding, tangled jungle, they advanced. By September 14, the Japanese were within 20-odd air miles of Port Moresby on what is known as the Imita Range. There the Australians held. There the terrain and Allied air attacks overcame the Japanese supply line from Buna.

Two weeks of stalemate followed. Behind the Allied lines

there was feverish activity. In Australia the 126th and 128th Infantry combat teams of the 32d U. S. Division were alerted. Less their artillery, they prepared to move.

September 25 found the 128th Infantry, and a detachment of the 126th Infantry, flown into Port Moresby. Three days later, when the remainder of the 126th arrived by boat, the 128th Infantry was opening a trail in the Goldie River Valley on the Australians' left flank.

As elements of the 126th Infantry on the right flank worked toward Juare over the almost impassable Kapa Kapa track, the Australians launched their counter attack on the Kokoda track. Slowly the Japanese fell back. Neither American force was in contact.

Meanwhile, an old landing strip at Wanigela, on the northeastern Papuan coast, was made serviceable by the Allied garrison there. By October 18, the 2d and 3d Battalions of the 128th Infantry had been flown into Wanigela.

From Wanigela, these units attempted the march over-land to Pongani but their forward elements found the Musa River Valley an impassable quagmire. The over-land plan was abandoned in favor of a ferry service incorporating small boats.

Two of these small boats off Pongani were bombed later by one of our own planes. The advance ground forces had not notified the Air Corps of the ferry service, and the pilot did not waste any time checking to make sure his targets were Japanese. Results: two killed and six wounded.

As the units at Wanigela were being ferried to Pongani, the Anti-Tank Company, the Cannon Company and the 2d Battalion of the 126th Infantry were moving overland from Moresby to Juare.

On November 2, two enemy transports were sighted 93 miles off Buna and were heavily attacked by our air units. One hit and several near misses were claimed. The convoy turned back. It was believed no troops landed.

On the same day, the Australians entered Kokoda. The Japanese had fallen back to Oivi. At Pongani a new strip was in operation and at Mount Sapia, to the south, another strip was nearing completion. Across the Solomon Sea, the Japanese, with complete disregard for their casualties, were hammering the Marine defenses on Guadalcanal. At Lae, Japanese air reinforcements were reported.

In the Buna-Oivi area the strength of the retreating enemy was now estimated at 4,000. Identifications gave the Oivi-Wairopi area the remnants of three battalions of the 144th Infantry, one battalion of pack artillery, a company of engineers and a part of one battalion of the 41st Infantry. In the Buna area it was believed that there were two battalions of the 41st Infantry and Line of Communication Troops.

2. Initial contact in The Buna Area.

By mid-November when General MacArthur authorized American patrolling to contact the enemy, all three battalions of the 128th Infantry were advancing up the coast from their base at Pongani. The 2d Battalion, 126th Infantry, was at Bofu with the remaining two battalions enroute to Bofu from Pongani. The Australians were crossing the Kumusi River at Wairopi in pursuit of the disorganized enemy in that area.

On the night of November 18 - 19, Japanese destroyers, reported to number four or five, and a Japanese cruiser were sighted off the coast north of Buna. Despite our air attacks, some enemy troops were landed.

Also, Japanese air power was coming into play. Between November 20 and the end of the month, scarcely a day passed that our troops were not bombed or strafed. In turn, our air was giving the

Japanese little respite.

During the night of November 19, elements of the Australian 25th Brigade entered Gona, only to withdraw because of a shortage of ammunition. (See Map "B").

Meanwhile, the 126th Infantry (less the 1st and 2d Battalions) crossed the Girua River and joined the Australian units moving on Soputa. They thereupon came under Australian command.

By November 20, elements of the 128th Infantry were reported in contact with the enemy on a line roughly located 700 yards south of Cape Endaiadere and running inland to the New Strip. The 1st and 3d Battalions, 128th Infantry, were on the line while the 1st Battalion, 126th Infantry, was in reserve.

While the Americans near the New Strip were feeling out the enemy positions in that area, the 2d Battalion, 128th Infantry, moved to Gerua Gardens on the track from Soputa. The 2d Battalion, 126th Infantry, followed. Enemy resistance was weak until the Americans neared Entrance Creek where the track forks, northwest to Buna Village and northeast to the coast below Buna Mission. Being held up here, the Americans moved into the swamp between the track and Girua River and, unopposed, advanced toward Buna Village. Near the Village they were stopped by prepared defensive positions.

Thus, ended the meeting engagement. The Girua River was the boundary between the two Allied Forces: the Seventh Australian Division, reinforced by the 126th U. S. Infantry (less two battalions), west of the river, was commanded by Major General G. A. Vasey; and the 32d U. S. Division (less the 127th Infantry, Division Artillery and elements of the 126th Infantry), east of the river, was commanded by Major General E. F. Harding. Both forces were part of the Advanced New Guinea Force, commanded by Lieutenant-General E. F. Herring of the Australian Army.

From the meeting engagement until the end of the month there was a virtual stalemate along the entire front. West of the Girua River, the enemy had taken up positions north of Soputa, on the Sanananda Track, and at Gona. They were on the only dry ground in the area and from these positions the enemy pinned down the swamp-ridden Seventh Australian Division.

East of the Girua River, the enemy was in strength behind prepared defenses organized in depth. These positions were also on dry ground and were placed so as to take full advantage of the terrain's canalization of any possible attack. Thus, was the 32d U. S. Division held up near Buna Village on the left and near the New Strip on the right.

During this stalemate, the Japanese, on the night of November 25 - 26, attempted to reinforce their Buna garrison. An unspecified number of enemy naval units were located north of Buna. Despite our continuous air attacks, the enemy landed some troops; however, it was believed they suffered heavy losses.

Again, on the night of November 27, the day the 127th Combat Team (less artillery) arrived in Port Moresby by boat, enemy naval units were reported off Buna--but this time our air search proved negative.

3. Summary of situation at the end of November.

By the end of November, the American Air Corps had successfully performed the prodigious job of moving thousands of American ground troops by air over mountainous jungle terrain. It had laid in limited supplies for the ground troops. It had made the Australian counterattack possible by its successful, though perilous, supply dropping in the misty, cragged reaches of the Kokoda track. It had continuously bombed and strafed Japanese positions. It had pared Japanese naval potentialities.

Unhappiest of November's hard realizations was the plight of the Buna ground forces. In this, their gruelling baptism of fire, they found the Japanese in perfect defensive positions. The Japanese left flank was based on the tidal, unfordable Girua River and Entrance Creek; their right flank was based on the sea as was their rear. To their front was thick jungle bogged into deep swamps traversed by tracks which canalized any American attack into narrow fronts against prepared positions.

Further, for weeks before initial contact, the Americans had fought the sapping heat, the mud, the weird night noises, the stench of the swamps, the jungle diseases. They were far from being fresh troops and were receiving no more than two lean meals per day.

The Allied supply picture was not bright. "Railheads" were newly constructed air strips at Dobodura and Popondetta except for the right flank force, south of Cape Endaiadere, which was supplied by small boats along the coast.

While the Air Force and the Transportation Corps were doing a good job moving requested supplies, the 32d Division had not announced a definite commitment on their daily minimum requirements.

Another unhappy reality was the weakening of the chain of command in the 32d Division. The terrain was, in itself, one unavoidable contributing factor, but the mixing of units could have been avoided. In some instances even platoons of different companies were under the same command.

The plight of the American ground forces was well known to the Commander-in-Chief of the Southwest Pacific Area, General Douglas MacArthur, as was the ever present possibility of an enemy reinforcement by sea.

Thus it was at midnight of November 29 - 30 when orders were received by Lieutenant General Robert L. Eichelberger, Commanding General, I Corps (US), to proceed by air transport from Rockhampton, Australia, to Port Moresby where he was to receive instructions relative to assuming command of the American and Allied troops in the Buna Area. (The artillery was Australian). General Eichelberger was authorized to bring an accompanying staff to include his Chief of Staff, six staff officers, his aide and nine enlisted men.

III OPERATIONS

1. First Break-Through to the Sea
   December 1 - 5

At 0958L 1 December, Lieutenant General Robert L. Eichelberger, Commanding General, I Corps (US), landed at Dobodura Strip #3. He was accompanied by his Chief of Staff, six staff officers, his aide and nine enlisted men. The previous night had been spent at Port Moresby where General Eichelberger and his accompanying staff had received instructions and a brief orientation.

At 1300L 1 December, General Eichelberger assumed command of the Buna Area.

The Division plans for an attack on December 2 were already in operation and were left untouched, while arrangements were completed to have the I Corps Assistants Chief of Staff G-2 and G-3 witness the attack on the right (in the New Strip area), and General Eichelberger on the left (in the Buna Village area).

During the night of December 1 - 2, Allied planes sighted and attacked enemy naval units landing troops just north of Buna. While our air attacks were vigorous, dawn disclosed 26 enemy landing barges on the beach near Sanananda. It was estimated that the enemy had successfully landed 1,000 troops.

The American ground attack of December 2 jumped off on schedule . . . but proved abortive. The Corps Commander personally witnessed the failure of the attack in the Buna Village area, and the I Corps Assistants Chief of Staff G-2 and G-3 witnessed the unenthusiastic feint in the New Strip area.

General MacArthur had told the Corps Commander he would find our forces "strong in the rear areas and weak in the forward areas". This proved true.

During December 3 - 4 the American forces were reorganized. General Harding, Division Commander, was relieved by Brigadier General Albert W. Waldron, former Division Artillery Officer; Colonel John W. Mott, commander of the American left flank force--hereafter to be known as the <u>Urbana Force</u>, was relieved by Colonel John E. Grose, I Corps Inspector General; and Colonel J. Tracey Hale, Jr., commander of the American right flank force--hereafter to be known as the <u>Warren Force</u>, was relieved by Colonel Clarence A. Martin, I Corps G-3.

Both Colonel Grose and Colonel Martin were Infantrymen and had had combat experience in the last war.

Units had been badly intermixed and were reformed. On the Urbana front, the 2d Battalion, 126th Infantry, was placed on the left and the 2d Battalion, 128th Infantry, on the right. On the Warren front, the 3d Battalion, 128th Infantry, was placed in the line extending from the south edge of the New Strip to the sea; and the 1st Battalion, 128th Infantry, in reserve, was placed behind the 3d Battalion, 128th Infantry. The 1st Battalion, 126th Infantry, was reformed south of the bridge between the Old and New Air Strips.

A 1/4-ton truck and 1-ton trailer at Dobodura. On December 5 the total motor transportation used by American forces in the Buna area numbered seven 1/4-ton trucks with three 1-ton trailers.

Also, during December 4, decisive steps were taken to finish investigation of supply installations and the correction of their shortcomings. Previously, our troops had not been receiving enough to eat.

At 1030L 5 December, following aerial, artillery and mortar preparations, the Warren and Urbana Forces jumped off in a coordinated attack. On both fronts, the attack met heavy resistance. Our artillery and mortar preparations had not neutralized enemy positions.

On the Warren front, five Bren Gun Carriers leading the attack were knocked out thirty minutes after the jump-off. Enemy resistance was concentrated in log barricades and bunkers, organized in depth and mutually supporting. Snipers were active. Throughout the day, the Warren Force determinedly hammered enemy positions, but by nightfall our gains were negative.

On the Urbana front, however, progress during the day was more encouraging. The enemy were in barricades and bunkers, but by dint of determined leadership our line advanced. A platoon of G Company, 126th Infantry, under command of Staff Sergeant Herman J. Bottcher, drove a wedge through to the sea between Buna Village and Buna Mission.

By 1630L, when orders for consolidation were issued, the Urbana left was pressed up tight against the enemy defenses around Buna Village, and well dug in along our corridor to the sea. On the Urbana right, we occupied the entire west bank of Entrance Creek with the one exception of The Coconut Grove, which constituted a dangerous reentrant in our lines with unlimited possibilities for reinforcement and attack by our enemies.

During the Urbana attack, General Waldron had been shot through the shoulder. The Corps Commander replaced him, in command of the forward elements of the 32d Division, with Brigadier General Clovis E. Byers, I Corps Chief of Staff.

In conclusion, the attack of December 5 established the strength and disposition of the enemy on the Warren front, and the isolation of Buna Village. Since the terrain and condition of troops in the Urbana Force precluded immediate assaults, continued pressure and advance by infiltration were ordered preliminary to the successive reduction of Buna Village, The Coconut Grove and The Island.

BUNA VILLAGE

F ⊠ 128 (-2)
2 Hvy MGs

E ⊠ 126
Can ⊠ 128
⊠ 128

G ⊠ 126

Scale 1:6,400
500 — 0 — 500 YDS.

BUNA VILLAGE

F ⊠ 2البا-2 P
1-37 MM
1 Plat. HMG
2-81 MM
1 Sec. LMG 128

Can ⊠ 128

2 ⊠ 128

Scale 1:6,400

500   0   500 YDS

BUNA MISSION
(GOV'T. STN.)

GIROPA PT.

Island

Entrance

Creek

Government Gardens

The Triangle

To Gerua Gardens

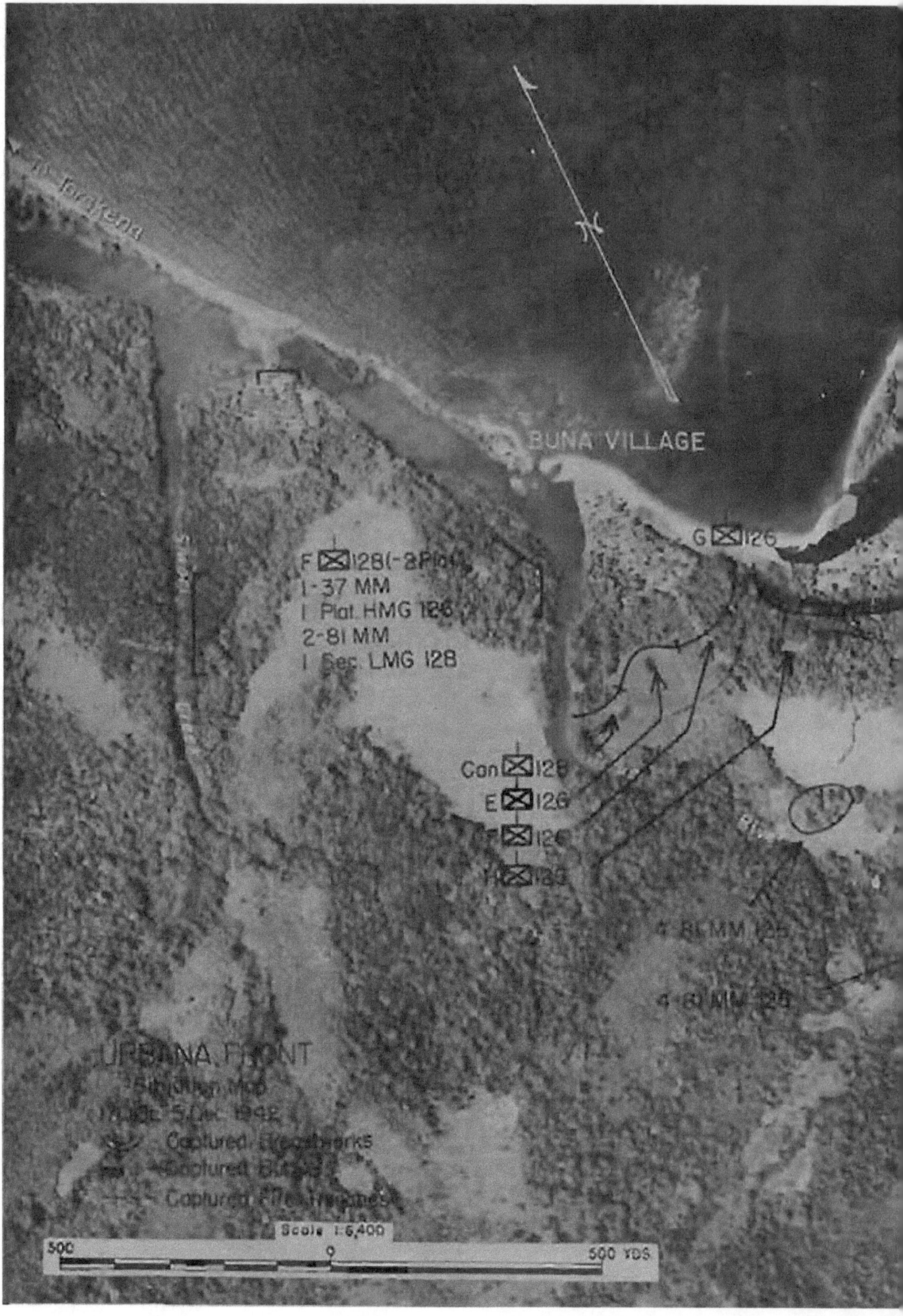

BUNA VILLAGE

Pt. Tarakena

F ⊠ 128(-2 Plat)
1-37 MM
1 Plat. HMG 126
2-81 MM
1 Sec. LMG 128

G ⊠ 126

Con ⊠ 128
E ⊠ 126
F ⊠ 126
H ⊠ 126

4-81 MM 126

4-81 MM 126

URBANA FRONT
Situation Map
Noon 5 Dec 1942
Captured Breastworks
Captured Bunkers
Captured Rifle Trenches

Scale 1:6,400
500   0   500 YDS

BUNA MISSION
(GOV'T. STN.)

GIROPA PT.

Government
Gardens

Island

Entrance

E ⊠ 128

Coconut Grove

The Triangle

G ⊠ 128

To Gerbo Gardens

STRIP PT.

Old Strip

WARREN FRONT
Situation Map
0800 1 Dec. 1942

STRIP PT.

Old Strip

WARREN FRONT
Situation Map
0800 5 Dec., 1942

2. Capture of Buna Village
December 6 - 14

The period of December 6 to, and including, December 13 was one of preparation for the vicious and persistent attacks starting on December 14.

During the period, the Advanced Echelon, Headquarters, I Corps (US) and Headquarters, 32d Division were merged into <u>Headquarters Buna Force (US)</u> under the command of General Eichelberger; and front line units were reorganized and energized. Rations were increased, patrolling became extensive. Daily, our lines inched forward to better positions from which to attack.

On the Urbana front the enemy was not complacent. Our line was a noose about the neck of Buna Village. Twice, the enemy from both the Village and Buna Mission attacked our corridor to the sea. Each time the attack was thrown back.

Also, during the period the supply situation was improved by reorganization and a conference, at which definite priorities were set up on definite daily minimum requirements; and the headquarters of the 126th Infantry was transferred by the G.O.C., New Guinea Forces, from the Sanananda to the Buna front.

In the Sanananda area (Australian command), the only change was the taking of Gona (December 9) by elements of the 21st and 25th Australian Brigades.

With the arrival of Headquarters, 126th Infantry, the Corps Commander placed Lieutenant Colonel Clarence M. Tomlinson, Regimental Commander, in command of the Urbana Force. The approximate effective strength of the Urbana Force was 55 officers and 1062 enlisted men, and the approximate effective strength of the Warren Force was 114 officers and 1955 enlisted men. (These strengths are based on figures quoted in the G-3 Periodic Report

0400L to 1700L 10 December, Headquarters, Buna Force (US).

Throughout the American sector, the morale of the troops was gradually improving. This morale increase is noteworthy in that it paralleled a slight increase in the malaria and dengue fever rate and the commencement of torrential nightly rains which turned the jungle into a miserable morass of sucking mud. Contributing factors to the improvement of morale were more aggressive leadership, more food and the arrival of elements of the 127th Infantry.

As these elements arrived at Dobodura and Popondetta by plane, they were moved to the vicinity of Ango for a short period of conditioning. By December 11, I and K Companies, 127th Infantry, were ready and put into the line around Buna Village, relieving the 2d Battalion, 126th Infantry.

To their rear, the mortars of the Urbana Force had been organized into batteries. Each battery had registered in and firing data had been plotted into fire control charts.

Thus, the stage was set for a coordinated attack on Buna Village at 0700L 14 December.

During the night of 13 - 14 December, our air reconnaissance again sighted an enemy convoy moving toward Buna. Bombing missions were dispatched; however, the enemy succeeded in landing an estimated 1000 troops near the mouth of the Mambare River and 200 near the mouth of the Kumusi River.

At 0700L, 14 December, I and K Companies, 127th Infantry, jumped off following mortar and artillery preparations on Buna Village. Enemy resistance was not strong and by 1000L the Village was ours. Most of the enemy had evacuated. Fifty enemy dead were buried.

Captured Japanese bunker in Buna Village

With Buna Village in hand, the Corps Commander now turned his attention to Buna Mission. However, before the Mission could be attacked it was necessary to protect the Urbana right flank from the dangerous enemy salient constituted by The Coconut Grove and The Triangle, 300 yards to the southeast, on opposite side of Entrance Creek.

Thus, the next mission of the Urbana Force became the capture of The Coconut Grove and The Triangle.

BUNA VILLAGE

⊠ 128 I-2
37 MM
Plat. HMG
2-81 MM
1 Sec LMG 128

K ⊠ 127

⊠ 127

Scale 1:6400
500   0   500 YDS

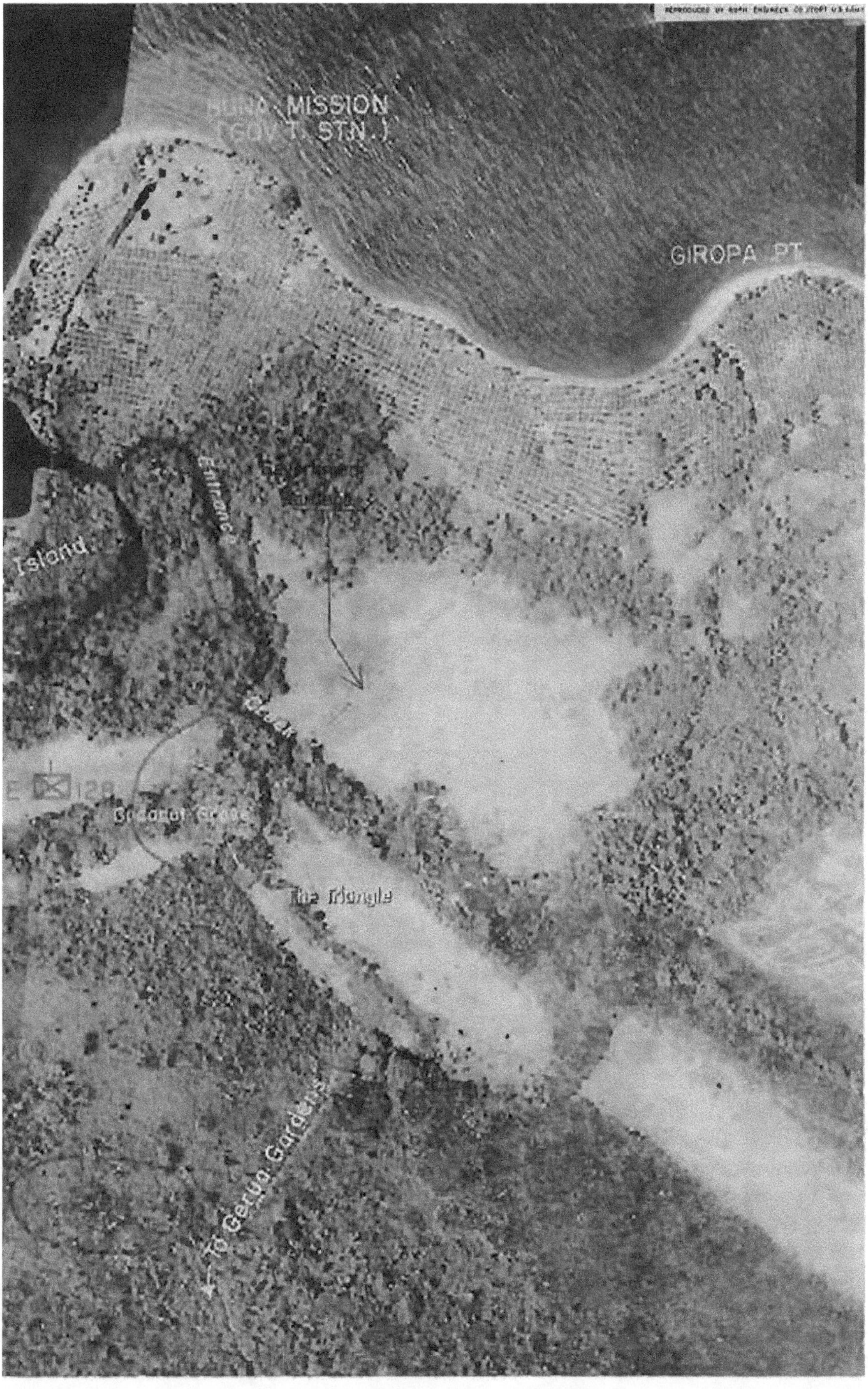
BUNA MISSION
(GOV'T. STN.)
GIROPA PT
Entrance
Island
Creek
128
Coconut Grove
The Triangle
To Gerua Gardens

BUNA VILLAGE

1281-2Bn
37 MM
1 Plat HMG 128
1 Sec. LMG 128

URBANA FRONT
Situation Map
1800L 14 Dec 1942
Captured Breastworks
Captured Bunkers
Captured Fire Trenches

Scale 1:6,400
500   0   500 YDS

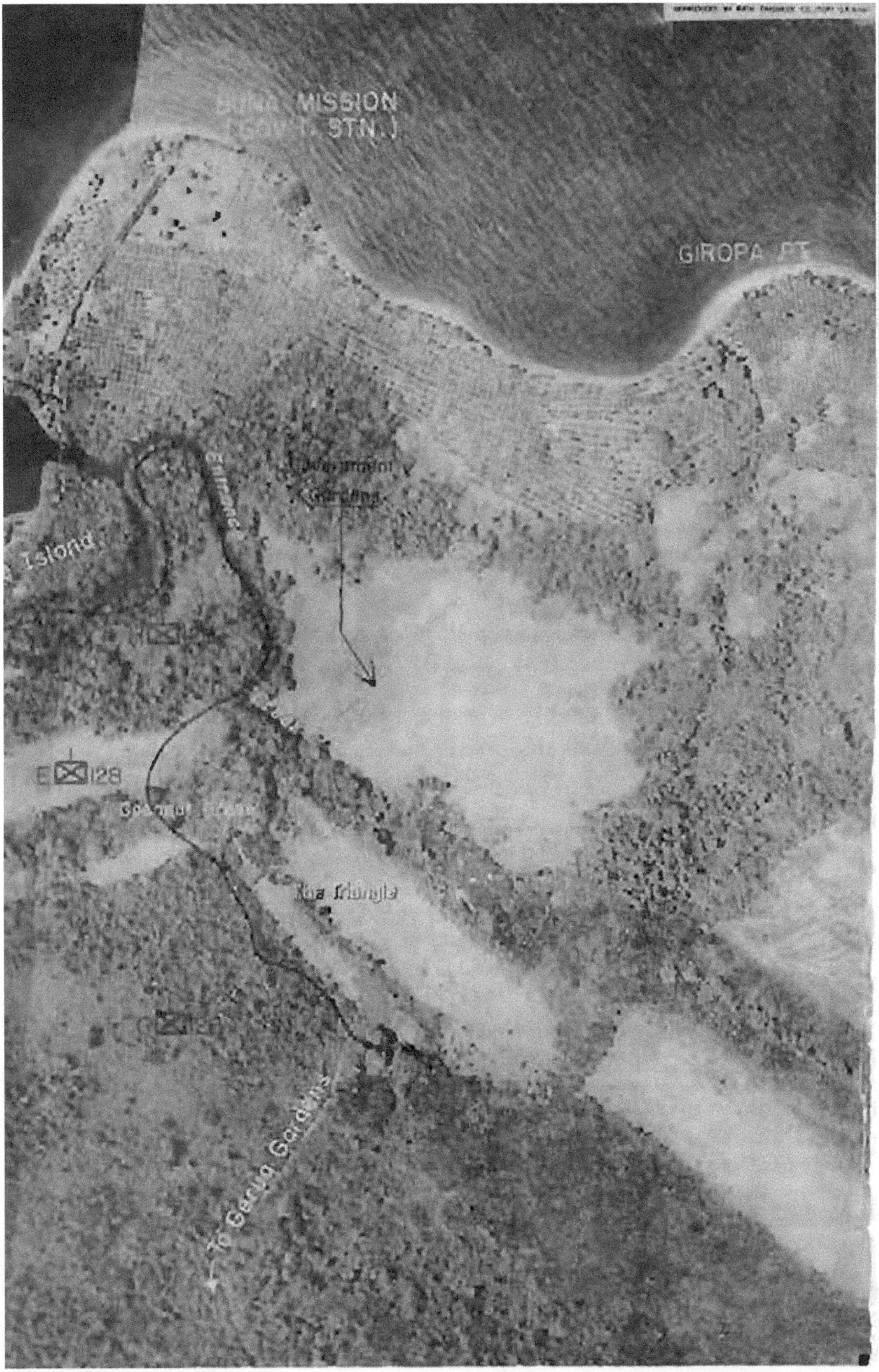

BUNA MISSION
(GOV'T. STN.)

GIROPA PT

Government
Gardens

Island

E 128

Coconut Grove

The Triangle

To Gerua Gardens

3. Capture of The Coconut Grove, and Preparation on Warren Front
December 15 - 17

The period of December 15 to, and including, December 17 was characterized by continuous attacks on the Urbana front, and preparation for attack on the Warren front.

The capture of Buna Village contributed to a high level of morale in the Urbana Force and, in order to exploit this condition, no time was lost in attacking The Coconut Grove on the west bank of Entrance Creek. At 1500L 16 December, a mortar and artillery preparation was placed on The Grove. Twenty minutes later, the preparation lifted and E and F Companies (less detachments), 128th Infantry, charged forward. However, their attack was short-lived for, again, our mortar and artillery preparation had failed to neutralize enemy positions.

General Byers had assisted in launching the attack and shortly after the jump-off was shot through the right hand.

By sundown, our troops managed to reach the edge of The Grove but were unable to enter it. Throughout the night, with its drenching rain, our troops clung to their positions and with dawn, December 17, charged and over-ran The Grove to kill 37 Japanese and take one prisoners--a wounded sergeant.

Now, only The Triangle remained to be eliminated before an attack could be launched to isolate Buna Mission by driving through to the sea between the Mission and Giropa Point.

G Company, 128th Infantry, had been containing The Triangle from the south and was given the mission of taking it out with the assistance of E Company, 128th Infantry, which was to attack from The Grove.

Each attack on The Triangle was preceded by heavy mortar fire with high explosives and smoke.

While G Company was attacking from the south, E Company established a shallow bridgehead across Entrance Creek southeast of The Grove. Enemy resistance was unexpectedly heavy. It had once been thought that The Triangle was held lightly, but E and G Companies by their attacks of December 16 - 17 definitely established that it was a carefully prepared defensive area.

General Eichelberger (with field glasses) studies Buna Mission from near Buna Village. Note beached enemy landing barges.

Determinedly, these two companies tried to advance, only to have their every move countered by heavy automatic weapon fire. Despite their best efforts, they failed to gain.

Meanwhile, on December 17 General Byers was evacuated and General Eichelberger assumed direct command of the 32d Division forward elements.

On the Warren Front during December 15 - 17, seven tanks (M-3s) of the 2/6 Australian Field Regiment and the 2/9 Australian Infantry Battalion of the 18th Australian Brigade, arrived via small boat.

The brigade commander, Brigadier George F. Wooten, being

senior to Colonel Martin, was made Warren Force commander by General Eichelberger on December 17, when the 18th Australian Brigade officially became part of Buna Force (US).

During the night of December 17, final arrangements were completed for a coordinated attack on the Warren front the following morning.

BUNA VILLAGE

128 (-2 Plat)
-37 MM
Plat. HMG 126
1 Sec. LMG 126

BUNA FRONT

Scale 1:6,400
500 0 500 YDS.

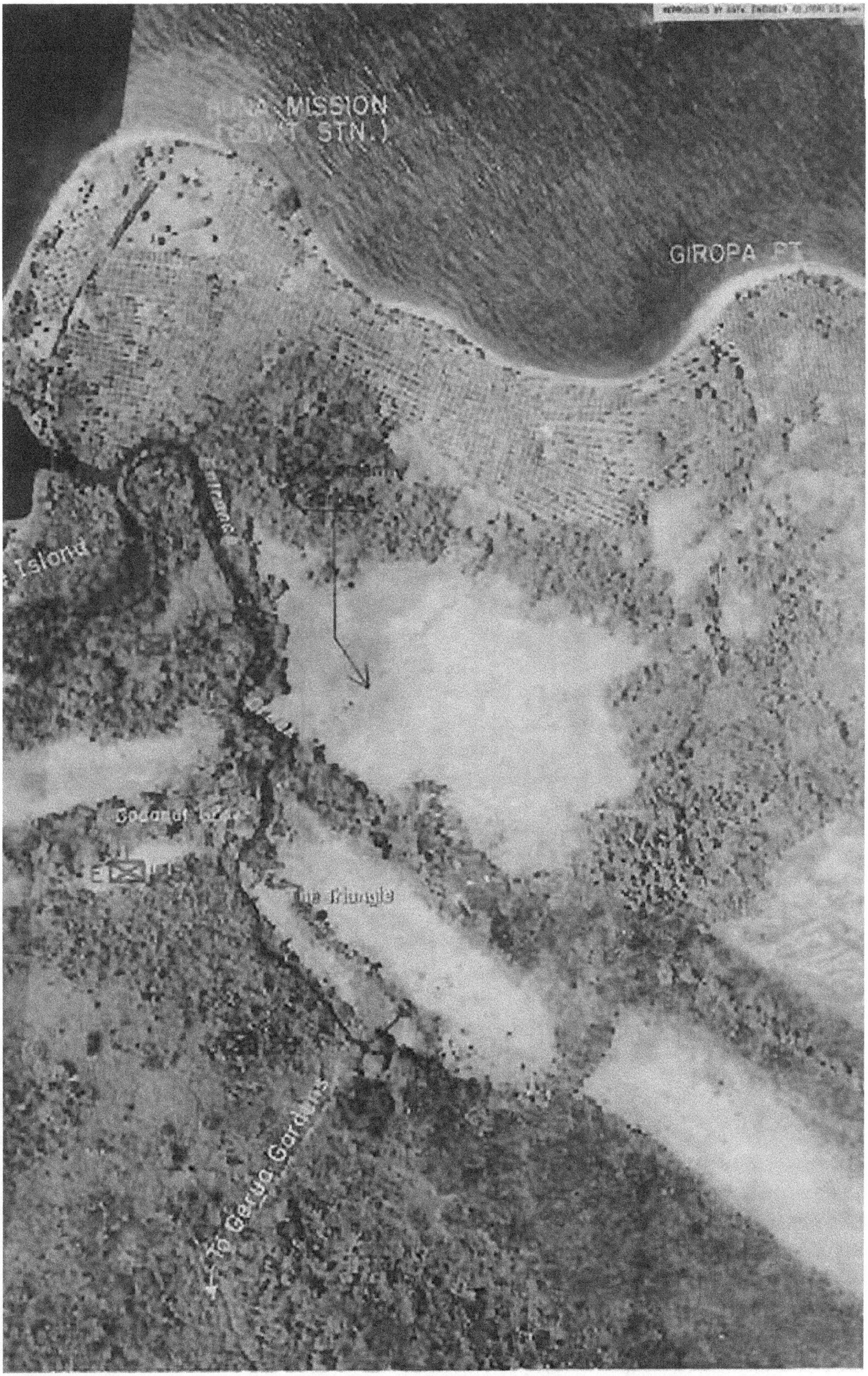

BUNA MISSION
(GOV'T STN.)

GIROPA PT

Island

Coconut

The Triangle

To Giropa Gardens

STRIP PT.

Old Strip

WARREN FRONT
Situation Map
1700L 17 Dec. 1942

4. Isolation of Buna Mission, and Attack on Warren Front
December 18 - 29

This period was characterized by persistent, bloody and desperate attacks which, despite heavy casualties and enemy resistance until death, set the stage for final victory east of the Girua River.

On the Urbana front between December 18 and December 20, the 2d Battalion, 126th Infantry, which had relieved G and E Companies, 128th Infantry, hammered valiantly but in vain against The Triangle. Every attack was thrown back by heavy enemy fire.

Track to The Triangle. Note bunker in background and vegetation.

Our lines were pressed up tight against the enemy positions, but in desperation artillery and mortar fire were called for. Again and again the artillery and mortar batteries hammered the enemy defenses . . . only to fail in the hoped-for neutralization of the Japanese bunkers.

On December 20, the depleted 2d Battalion, 126th Infantry, was relieved by E Company, 127th Infantry; and Colonel Grose, who was now Regimental Commander of the 127th Infantry, was placed in command of the Urbana Force. After a heavy artillery concentration, E Company attacked . . . only to be thrown back. The Buna Force Commander (General Eichelberger), in recognition of the impregnability of the position, then directed that The Triangle be contained, and proceeded with the execution of his plans for the attack on Buna Mission.

The first step was to drive a corridor through to the sea and isolate the Mission. During December 21, 22 and 23, K and I Companies, 127th Infantry, after crossing Entrance Creek at night under fire, struggled to enlarge the shallow bridgehead on the western side of the Government Gardens. Enemy resistance was stiff; every crossing of the unfordable stream drew heavy enemy fire; every inch on the east bank was sorely contested. Yet, by December 23, the two companies had enlarged the bridgehead sufficiently for an attack by the 2d Battalion, 127th Infantry, the following morning.

Meanwhile, on the night of December 22 - 23, F Company, 127th Infantry, had succeeded in taking The Island in Entrance Creek.

South bridge from The Island to mainland. Note jungle.

During the night of December 23 - 24, L Company, 127th Infantry, moved in position to spearhead the attack across the Gardens, which is perhaps best described by an extract from a letter written by the Buna Force Commander to General MacArthur:

> "I think the all time low of my life occurred yesterday (December 24). We had seven line companies available and I had given five of them to Grose to attack but when the rolling barrage started his troops bogged down in the kunai grass, which is about five feet high. He was unable to get reports back from L Company, one platoon of which did go through and arrive at the beach. His right company, I Company, bogged down almost at once . . . Instead of pushing through with a power drive as I had instructed . . . thinking his whole force had bogged down, he delayed his advance. When he found the platoon of L Company had gone through he pushed K Company in. K Company did not acquit itself well and only one officer and eight men went through. As a consequence the platoon of L Company which reached the beach . . . retired."

The attack was renewed on December 25. Contrasting with all previous attacks on the Urbana front, the attack was not preceded with an artillery and mortar preparation but rather with diversionary fire from The Island. While this attack made some headway, enemy resistance was still such that we were stopped short of the beach.

The attacks were continued, but without success. On December 28, the Buna Force Commander directed an attack using assault boats from The Island. The plan called for the landing of troops on the Mission side of the Creek to cover the repair of the bridge from The Island, after which our troops on The Island were to attack across the bridge.

The attack failed, however, when the assault boats landed under heavy enemy fire on the American side of the Creek.

Meanwhile, on December 28, E Company, 127th Infantry, which had been containing The Triangle, found enemy resistance dissipating and attacked successfully. Most of the enemy had evacuated from the area which was found to be an intricate network of 18 bunkers and connecting fire trenches, largely surrounded by swamps, making understandable the difficulty of its capture.

Japanese fire trenches and bunker in The Triangle.

On December 29, the attack was renewed through the Gardens and this time went through to the sea. By late afternoon our troops were established in well dug-in positions along a corridor reaching across the Gardens and including from 200 to 400 yards of the coast between Buna Mission and Giropa Point.

On the Warren front, the period December 18 - December 29 was also a period of important gains. On December 18, seven M-3 tanks of the 2/6 Australian Field Regiment, followed by the 2/9 Battalion of the 18th Australian Brigade, attacked north through the coconut plantation toward Cape Endaiadere, passing through the 3d Battalion, 128th Infantry, which followed in their rear mopping up. On the left, the 1st Battalion, 128th Infantry, wheeled to the west and closely supported the 2/9 Battalion. By the end of the attack, our line ran roughly in a northerly direction from the eastern end of the New Strip to a point on the coast 600 yards west of Cape Endaiadere.

The attack was heavily opposed. Three of the tanks were knocked out and Australian infantry casualties were high. The network of enemy positions was found to be even more formidable than our patrols had indicated. Bunkers and log barricades were numerous and connecting fire trenches and sniper-posts were a constant source of trouble.

After reorganizing on December 19, the attack was continued on December 20. By the end of the day, our line ran from a point on the coast 500 yards west of Strip Point, southwest to Sinemi Creek and down the Creek to a point just north of the bridge between the strips, and then due south across the New Strip about 150 yards from the bridge.

From left to right, the line was now held by the 1st Battalion, 126th Infantry; the 1st Battalion, 128th Infantry; the 3d Battalion, 128th Infantry and the 2/9 Australian Infantry Battalion.

Tank knocked out in front of log barricade and bunkers in the coconut plantation.

On December 21, the Warren Force reorganized while patrols searched along Sinemi Creek for a suitable crossing. This was found during the ensuing night just north of the dispersal bays at the southeastern end of the Old Strip. The 2/10 Australian Infantry Battalion established a bridgehead over which three companies were moved December 23. During December 23, the 1st Battalion, 126th Infantry, attacked down the New Strip and at 1230L overran the now famed bridge between the strips to continue its advance and joined the 2/10 Battalion in a line, facing west, 300 yards across the Old Strip.

The 1st Battalion, 128th Infantry, was now dropped back in reserve near the bridge between the strips where four tanks were waiting while the bridge was repaired, under fire, by American engineers and infantry.

On December 24, the tanks attacked up the northeastern side of the Old Strip in support of the 2/10 Battalion; while the 1st Battalion, 126th Infantry, attacked across the strip and then up its southwestern side abreast the 2/10 Battalion. Enemy resistance was from scattered positions on each side of the strip and from a system of bunkers, at the northwestern end of the strip, from which the Japanese were delivering machinegun and dual-purpose AA fire on our ground troops.

During December 25 - December 28, the line inched forward, infiltrating enemy positions and knocking them out one at a time. By 1600L December 29, the right of the line was based on Sinemi Creek about 800 yards from the mouth. From this point, the line ran southwest to bend in an arc around the dispersal bays at the northwestern end of the strip and then due west for about 750 yards. In order, from left to right, the line was held by C and A Companies, 2/10 Battalion; C and A Companies, 128th Infantry; C Company, 126th

Infantry; and B and D Companies, 2/10 Battalion.

Enemy bunkers near bridge between Old and New Strips.

Meanwhile, deep in the Warren rear area, the 2/12 Australian Infantry Battalion and eleven M-3 tanks of the 2/6 Australian Field Regiment were moving toward the front.

Thus ended the period December 18 through December 29. The stage was now set for the Buna Force Commander to launch his final attacks east of the Girua River.

The bridge between the Old and the New Strips.

BUNA VILLAGE

⊠ 126 (-2 Rfl)
1 - 37 MM
1 Plat. HMG 126
1 Sec. LMG 126

URBANA FRONT
Situation Map
1200, 30 Dec 1942
Captured Breastworks
Captured Bunkers
Captured Fire Trenches

Scale 1:8,400
500　0　500 YDS

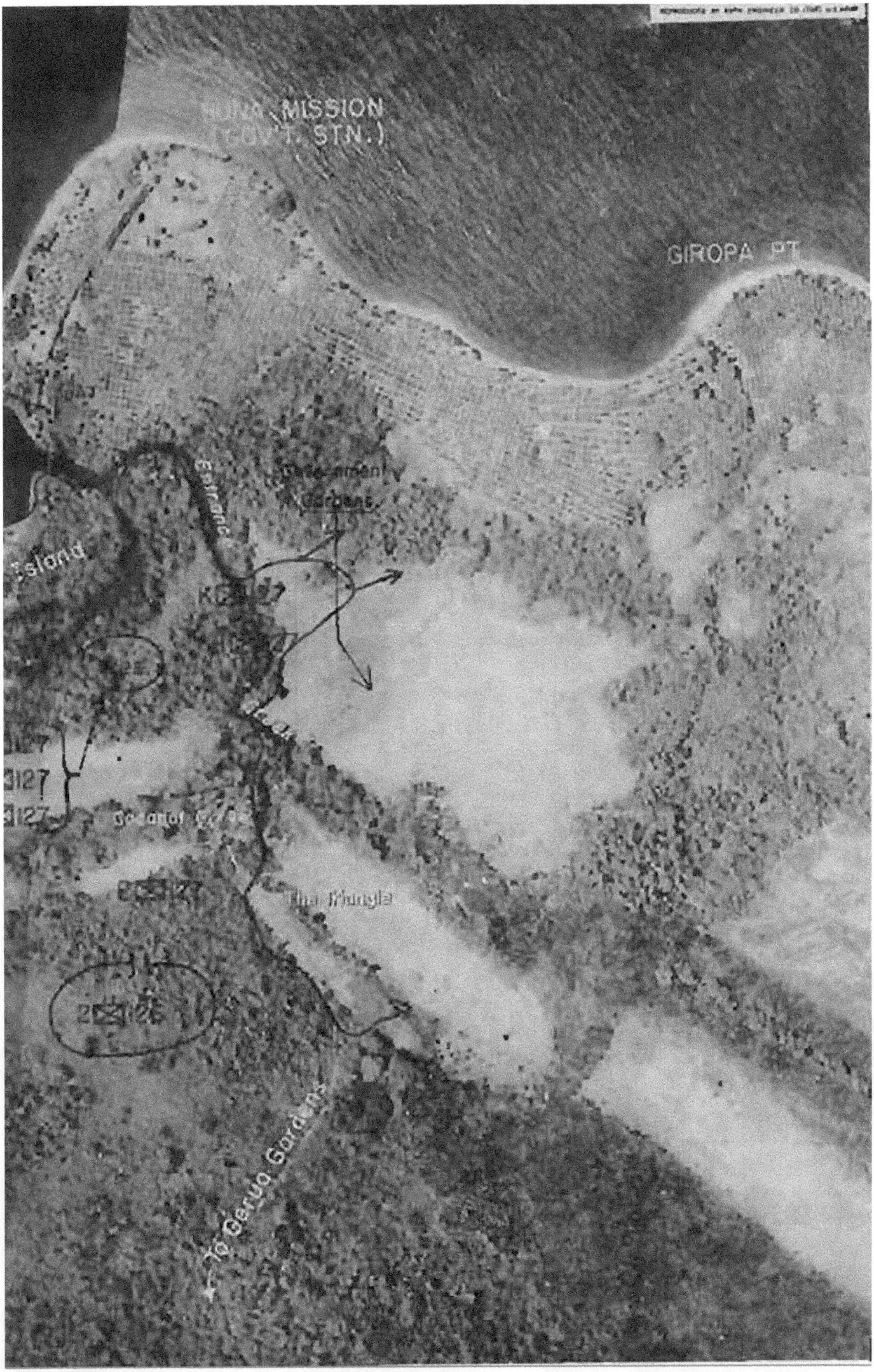

BUNA MISSION (GOV'T. STN.)

GIROPA PT.

Entrance

Government Gardens

Island

Coconut Grove

The Mungle

To Geruo Gardens

BUNA VILLAGE

⊠ 128 (—
— 37 MM
Plat HMG
Sec LMG

URBANA POINT

Scale 1:6,400
500   0   500 YDS

BUNA MISSION
(GOV'T. STN.)

GIROPA PT.

Government
Gardens

Coconut Grove

To Gcoga Gardens

STRIP PT.

Old Strip

WARREN FRONT
Situation Map
2000L 18 Dec. 1942
Captured Breastworks
Captured Bunkers
Captured Gun Trenches

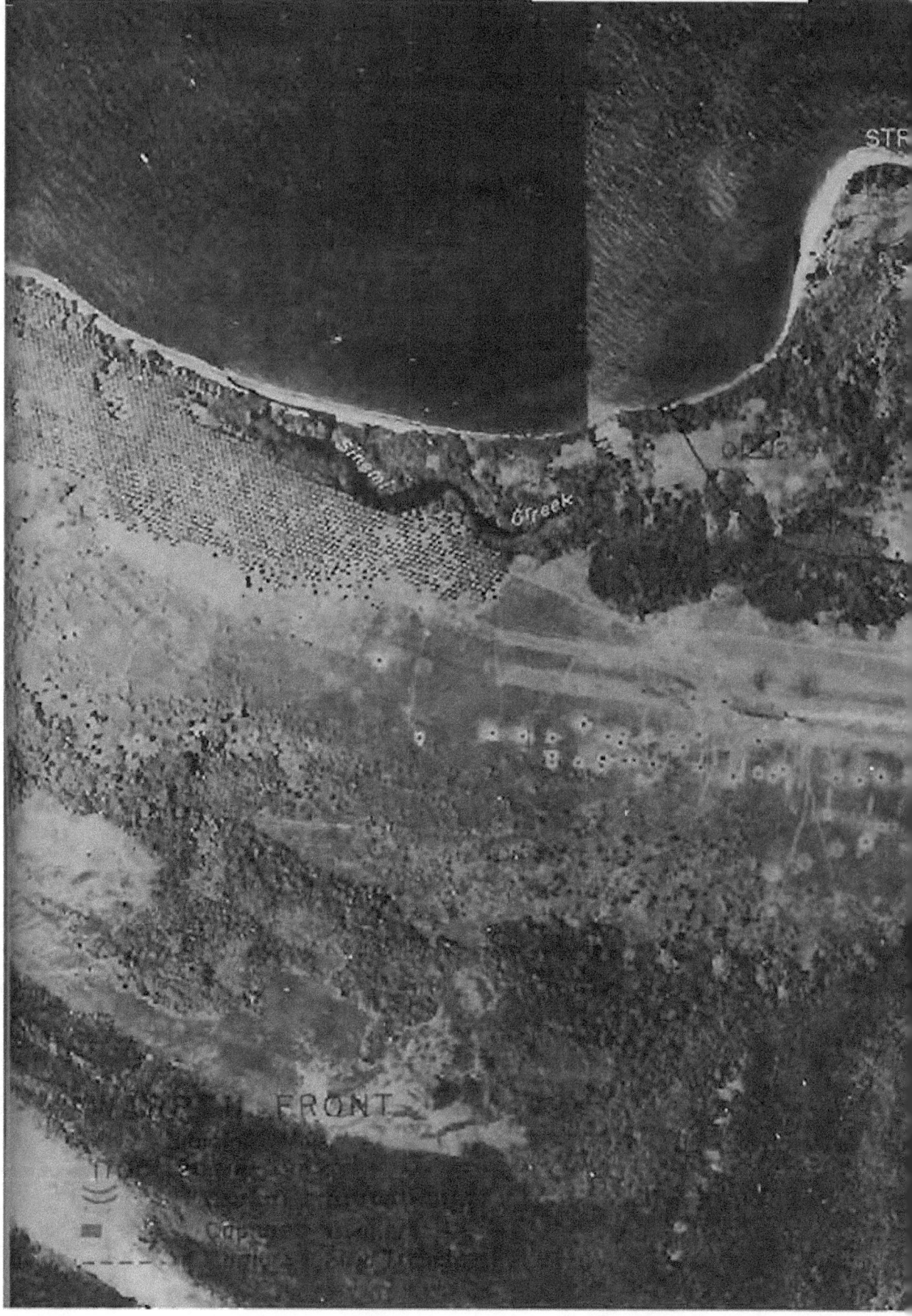

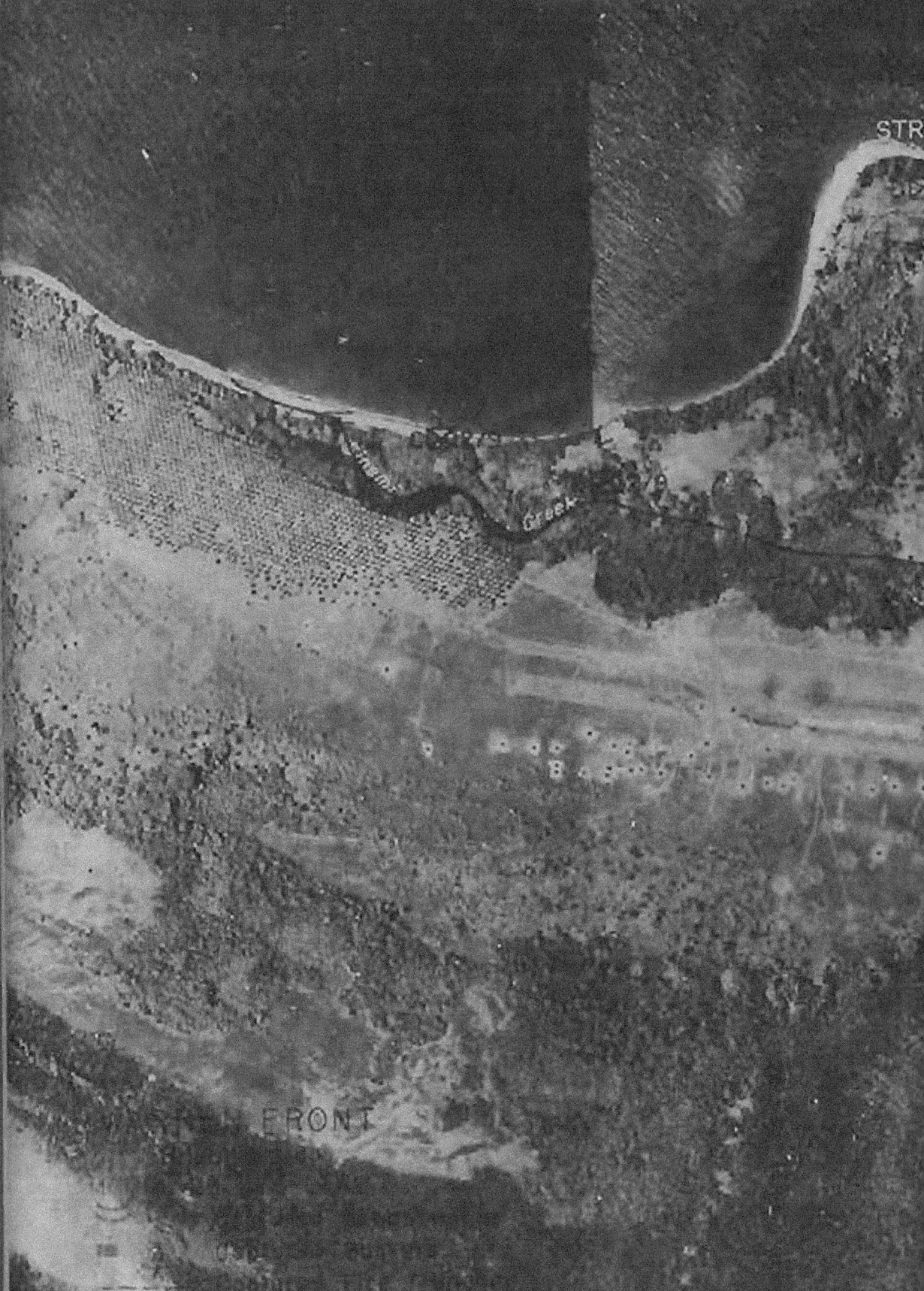

STR

2/9 ⊠ 2/9

⊠ 2/10

C ⊠ 2/10   A ⊠ 2/10   ⊠ 128   B ⊠ 2/10

C ⊠ 126

WOLF DEN FRONT

5. Capture of Buna Mission
December 30 - January 5

This was the period of victory east of the Girua River.

On the Urbana front during December 30, the corridor isolating Buna Mission was gradually enlarged.

On December 31, at 0430L, E Company, 127th Infantry, and F Company, 128th Infantry, pushed across the mouth of Entrance Creek and established positions on the sand spit west of Buna Mission.

During the same day, the depleted 2d Battalion, 126th Infantry, attacked beyond The Triangle to advance 300 yards to the east. By nightfall, we held the whole of the Government Garden area, and one of our patrols operating to the southeast established contact with the Warren Force left.

On January 1, G Companies, 127th and 128th Infantry, moved into position in the corridor in preparation for an attack January 2. While these companies were moving in, C Company, 127th, on the left of the corridor pushed forward some 150 yards.

The attack of January 2 was preceded by artillery and mortar fire, after which the infantry moved forward from the northwestern side of the corridor toward Buna Mission. Progress was slow; there was heavy cross-fire from the numerous enemy bunkers. G Company, 127th Infantry, spearheaded the attack with G Company, 128th Infantry, in support. Other supporting elements in the attack were A, C, F, I and L Companies, 127th Infantry, and, from the spit, F Company, 128th Infantry. Despite determined enemy resistance, the attack continued to gain momentum, finally over-running Buna Mission.

Of the attack, General Eichelberger wrote:

> "At 4:30 P.M. I crossed the bridge (from The Island) after C Company had passed and I saw American troops with their bellies out of the mud and their eyes in the sun circling unafraid around the bunkers. It was one of the grandest sights I have ever seen . . the 127th Infantry found its soul . . . "

General Eichelberger crossing from The Island to Buna Mission.

With the Mission in hand, C Company, 127th Infantry, was moved in support of B Company, 127th Infantry, to attack toward Giropa Point from the southeastern side of the corridor. The attack was a success and by nightfall the Buna Force Commander controlled the entire coastline east of the Girua River.

On Buna Mission proper, 190 enemy were buried. There was no count taken of the number of enemy who attempted to swim out to sea only to be picked off by our troops. Some enemy, no doubt, escaped into the swamps while others were buried without count in demolished bunkers. (For a count of enemy dead, etc., see ORDER OF BATTLE).

On the Warren front during December 30 - 31, there was a general reorganization, after which an attack supported by eleven M-3 tanks was launched toward Giropa Point. The attack jumped off at 0800L 1 January and at 0930L reached the coast between Giropa Point and the mouth of Sinemi Creek.

The attack had not been heavily opposed; only one tank was

knocked out and our casualties were light. By nightfall only two pockets of enemy resistance remained on the Warren front: one between the northeast dispersal bays and the mouth of the creek, and the other in the swamp area about 300 yards south of the Giropa Creek mouth.

During January 2, these pockets were attacked and on January 3 they were wiped out.

The attack of January 1 had been led by the 2/12 Australian Infantry Battalion and the 1st Battalion, 128th Infantry, supported by the 3d Battalion, 128th Infantry, and the 2/10 Australian Infantry Battalion.

The enemy pocket south of Giropa Creek mouth was wiped out by the 1st Battalion, 128th Infantry; and the pocket in the dispersal bay area, by the 3d Battalion, 128th Infantry.

Thus ended the fighting east of the Girua River. For many days after the last organized resistance had been broken on January 3, enemy stragglers were ferreted out and killed or captured (mostly killed) by the troops of Buna Force (US). Upon completion of mopping up, these forces were assigned beach defense missions, with the exception of the 127th Infantry and the 18th Australian Brigade which were to assist in the neutralization of enemy resistance west of the Girua River.

BUNA MISSION
(GOV'T. STN.)

GIROPA PT.

The Island

K

M ⊠ 127

G ⊠ 127
B ⊠ 127

G ⊠ 127
G ⊠ 128

2 ⊠ 126
Government
Gardens

Coconut Grove

to Gerua Gardens

STRIP PT

BUNA VILLAGE

To Tarakena

Swoci Creek

Girua River

BUNA DEFENSE PLAN (JAPANESE)
As compiled at the end of the campaign.
Breastworks
Bunkers
Fire Trenches
Barbed Wire
Anti-Aircraft Positions

Scale 1:6,400
500   0   500 YDS.

the 2/6 Australian Field Regiment were transferred from Buna to the Sanananda front north of Soputa. Also, elements of the 163 Infantry, 41st U. S. Division, began arriving from Port Moresby by air.

On January 12, elements of the 18th Brigade supported by the tanks of the 2/6 Field Regiment attacked north of Soputa, but met heavy resistance which knocked out all three tanks and rendered the attack abortive.

On the following day, General Eichelberger was placed in command of Advance New Guinea Forces including all Allied troops north of the Owen Stanley Range. Vigorous patrolling was at once directed in an effort to obtain a more accurate picture of the Japanese positions. The patrols operating through the swamps caught the enemy at the beginning of a withdrawal. An Allied attack was immediately ordered. Allied troops were then able to wipe out all the Japanese area which had so long held up the Allied advance.

The 18th Brigade pushed rapidly up the Cape Killerton track meeting slight resistance; and the 163d Infantry drove forward up the Sanananda track and developed the enemy's main pocket of resistance approximately 2200 yards south of Sanananda. By January 15 the enemy area north of the road block was mopped up.

On reaching the coast, elements of the 18th Brigade attacked to the east and on January 18, reached Giruwa, where it met the 127th Infantry which had fought its way up the coast from Tarakena.

The 163d Infantry continued its attacks against the enemy pocket on the Sanananda track until the afternoon of January 21 when they were able to report that the Japanese were softening rapidly. By January 22, all organized enemy resistance west of the Girua River was wiped out.

During the campaign on the Sanananda front (including Gona), approximately 3000 enemy were killed and 130 taken prisoner. The

great majority of the enemy had fought on the Kokoda trail and were ravaged by hunger and disease. Their morale, according to prisoners of war, was thoroughly shattered when, on the night of January 16 - 17, their high command removed wounded from a barge in which they were to be evacuated . . . and themselves departed leaving their troops the sole honor of "a glorious death".

IV ORDER OF BATTLE

1. <u>Enemy</u>.

<u>General</u>.--No effort will be made in this report to trace the enemy chain of command because conclusive evidence is not available. Of relative information in hand, two facts stand out: it seems fairly conclusive that the supreme commander of Japanese troops in New Guinea was (and is at the time of writing) Major General Oda; and that he succeeded Major General Tomitaro Horii who drowned when his raft turned over on the flooded Kumusi River during the retreat from Wairopi in November.

<u>Identifications</u>.--The Japanese left flank in the Cape Endaiadere area was held principally by the 3d Battalion, 229th Regiment, with an estimated strength of 465, and the Yamamoto Butai with an approximate strength of 300.

The Japanese right flank in the Buna Village area was held principally by two Marine groups: the Yasuda Butai and the Tsukioka Butai. Their combined minimum strength is estimated at 400.

Attached to the above flank units and filling out the remainder of the Japanese perimeter were elements of other units including a heavy anti-aircraft unit, tentatively identified as the 73d Independent Unit, with a minimum strength of 100; a battery of mountain artillery thought to be from the 3d Battalion, 55th Field Artillery and numbering not less than 100 troops; some remnants of the 144th Infantry totaling about 100; a minimum of 300 miscellaneous troops including engineer, medical, signal, and supply personnel; and approximately 400 laborers of the 14th and 15th Construction units.

Collectively speaking the Japanese troops in the sector were thoroughly seasoned campaigners. Further, they were largely fresh troops, with the exception of certain elements, in that they had not taken part in the drive on Port Moresby and the subsequent retreat.

Brief Histories.

3d Battalion, 229th Infantry Regiment.--This unit was commanded by Major Haihachi Kimmotsu and was known as the Kimmotsu Butai. It was a part of the 38th Division and had seen previous action near Canton and later at Hong Kong. The regiment arrived in Rabaul from Java on October 30, 1942. From Rabaul the 1st and 2d Battalions were sent to Guadalcanal and the 3d Battalion to the Buna coast where it landed November 18th.

Yamamoto Butai.--This unit was commanded by Col. Hiroshi Yamamoto. It left Japan in early October as a part of a replacement section numbering 1000 officers and enlisted men for the 144th Regiment (Kusunose Butai), which had been decimated in the Owen Stanley Range. The unit arrived in Rabaul on October 30, 1942. Shortly thereafter, Col. Yamamoto was ordered with a detachment of 300 to the Buna combat zone. They arrived on approximately November 13. The plan was for Col. Yamamoto to assume command of the 144th Regiment, Col. Kusunose having become a casualty. However, on Yamamoto's arrival he was instructed to take a part of his detachment to the Buna - Cape Endaiadere sector. There he was placed in command of all Army units and instructed to cooperate with Col. Yasuda of the Naval force (Marines). The replacements in the Yamamoto Butai were well trained and, with individual exceptions, experienced in many of Japan's previous campaigns including the Philippines, China, Malaya, etc.

Yasuda Butai.--This unit was commanded by Col. Yoshitatsu Yasuda. It was a Naval Force (Marines) and while definite identification is lacking, it is known that the men of the unit had fought in China, Malaya, Singapore and in various islands of the South and

Southwest Pacific Area. The unit had been in Buna for several months before contact with the Americans was made in the latter part of November. Beside the Marines, Col. Yasuda commanded the elements of the 14th and 15th Construction units in the Buna - Cape Endaiadere area.

14th Construction unit.--Little is known about this unit except that it is believed to have been predominantly Japanese coolie labor. It came to Buna in August. However, there are credible indications that a large part of it was withdrawn to Giruwa during the latter part of October, leaving only a detachment of 200 in the Buna area.

15th Construction unit.--This unit was commanded by Naval Technician Atsushi. It arrived at Rabaul August 5, 1942. It included 102 Japanese laborers as section leaders, some Chinese, 500 Formosans and 1500 Korean laborers. It left Rabaul August 11 and landed in the Buna area August 13. The 500 Formosans were attached to an Army unit at Gona and the remainder of the unit was sent to Buna on August 18 to work on the air strips. On August 28, most of the unit was ordered to Giruwa to construct a road to Port Moresby, leaving only 230 in Buna. Of these 230, forty-two were Japanese and the remainder Koreans.

Strength:--The enemy's strength in the Buna area (Buna Village - Cape Endaiadere) was approximately 2200 at the time of the meeting engagement. Of this number, 1450 were buried or captured by our troops during the campaign. The remainder may be accounted for as (1) buried by the enemy, (2) evacuated by barge because of wounds or disease, (3) killed while trying to escape out to sea on rafts, small boats or by swimming, (4) sealed uncounted in caved-in bunkers, and (5) escaping through the swamps to the Sanananda area.

2. **Allied.**

<u>General</u>.--Heading the Allied chain of command in the Buna Campaign was General MacArthur, Commander-in-Chief, SWPA, with Advanced General Headquarters in Port Moresby. The next lower link was General Sir Thomas Blamey, who performed the dual role of GOC, Land Forces, SWPA, and GOC, New Guinea Force with headquarters at Port Moresby.

The combined American and Australian troops north of the Owen Stanley Range were under Lieutenant General E. F. Herring, GOC, Advanced New Guinea Force, with headquarters initially near Soputa. Late in December, 1942, this headquarters was moved to the east bank of the Samboga River near Dobodura.

Under Advanced New Guinea Force the chain of command led to the two Allied Forces in the forward area: west of the Girua River, Major General G. A. Vasey commanded the Seventh Australian Division reinforced by part of the 126th Infantry (US) in the Sanananda - Gona area; and east of the Girua River, until December 1, were elements of the 32d U. S. Division. On December 1, Lieutenant General Eichelberger commanding I Corps (US) assumed command of the troops in the zone east of the Girua, with the I Corps (US) Advanced Headquarters near Henahamburi. On December 7, Headquarters, I Corps (US) and Headquarters, 32d U. S. Division were merged to create Headquarters, Buna Force (US) which was commanded by Lieutenant General Eichelberger until the end of the campaign.

Buna Force (US) was divided into three elements: the Urbana Force on the left flank in the Buna Village - Buna Mission area; the Warren Force on the right flank in the Cape Endaiadere area; and the Alma Force which was the service of supply.

After the fall of Buna Mission, General MacArthur returned to General Headquarters, SWPA, in Australia with the members of his advanced headquarters and General Blamey returned to Land Headquarters, SWPA, also in Australia. As a result of their departures from the combat area, Lieutenant General Herring became GOC, New Guinea Force at Port Moresby and Lieutenant General Robert L. Eichelberger became GOC, Advanced New Guinea Force with headquarters near Dobodura.

Charts #1 and #2 (following page 47) give a graphical presentation of the Buna Force (US) chain of command, including the composition of forces.

Brief Histories:

The 32d U. S. Division, a National Guard unit from Michigan and Wisconsin, was inducted into Federal Service October 15, 1940, and sent to Camp Beauregard, Louisiana.

In February, 1941, the division was moved to Camp Livingston, Louisiana. It participated in the Louisiana Maneuvers of 1941, was alerted in February, 1942, and sent to Fort Devens, Massachusetts. Shortly after its arrival at Fort Devens, the division was ordered overland to the San Francisco area. It arrived in Australia April 22, 1942.

Between the time the division was inducted and sent overseas, it supplied the usual cadres and received Selective Service replacements. It had a small percentage of reserve officers and the authorized quota of regular officers.

After twice being moved in Australia, the division (less its artillery) was sent to New Guinea with the last elements arriving in November. The Buna Campaign was its first combat experience.

The 163d U. S. Infantry, 41st U. S. Division, was a National Guard regiment from Montana inducted into Federal Service September 16, 1940. While in the United States its home station was Fort Lewis, Washington. Along with the remainder of the division it supplied many cadres until just before the outbreak of the war. Following the opening of hostilities the division was on coastal defense work in the Northwest Pacific area. The 163d Infantry arrived in Australia April 6, 1942, and was sent to New Guinea in mid-December.

The Sanananda Campaign was the first combat experience for the 163d Infantry. Other elements of the 41st Division did not participate in the Sanananda Campaign which ended officially on January 22, 1943.

The Seventh Australian Division and the 18th Australian Brigade had seen previous action. Units of each force had fought in Greece, Crete, Syria and North Africa.

Strength Reports.--For data concerning strength of American units see Appendix, Annex #1, G-1 Report. For battle losses see Appendix, Annex #4, Inclosure E, Medical Report.

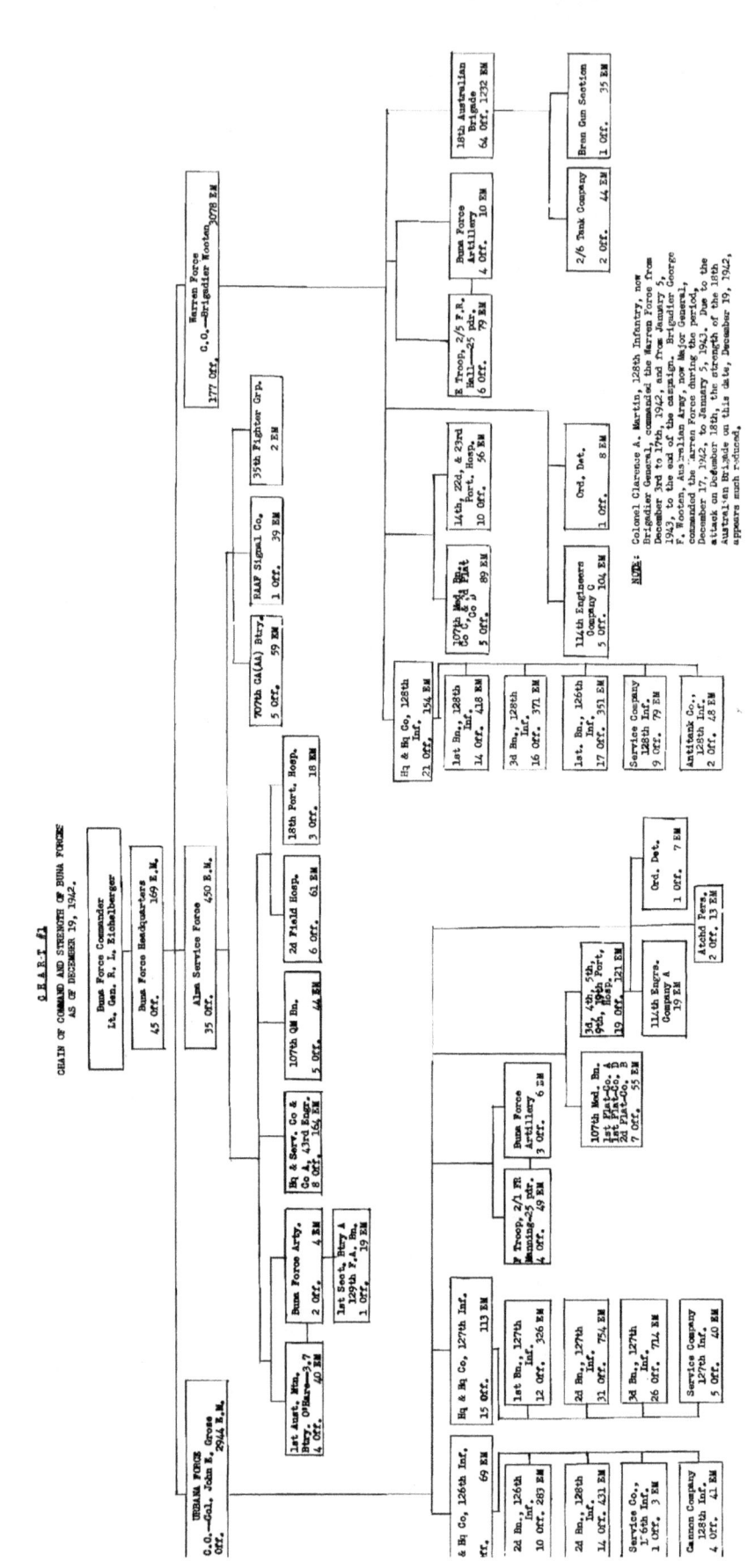

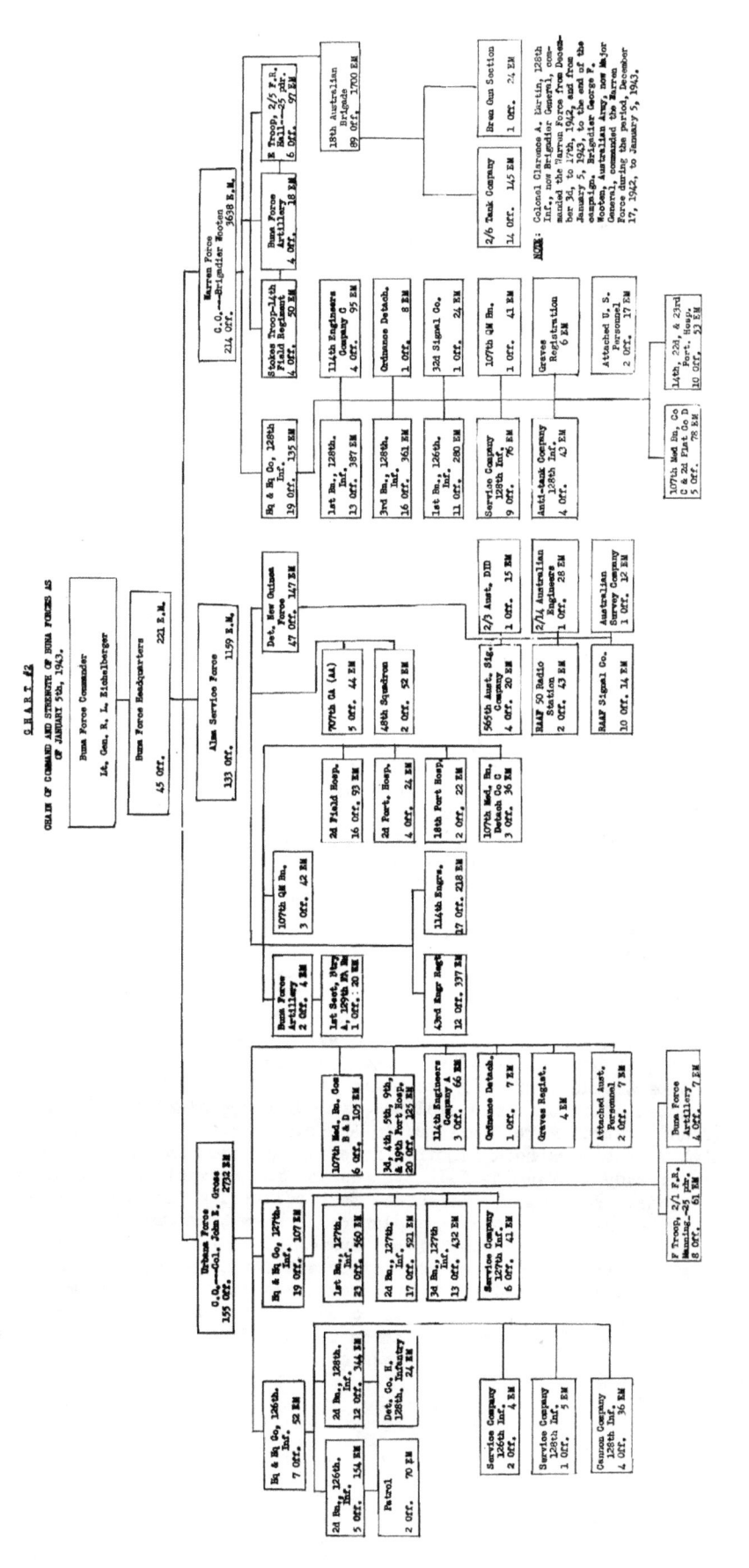

APPENDIX

ANNEX #1

G-1 Report

I. <u>TERRAIN</u>---

In connection with the general terrain study, attention is particularly invited to the peculiar conditions making it necessary for the Buna Forces to operate in two (2) wings, the Warren and Urbana Forces, with no center, and also to the tenuous line of communications to each of these wings.

II. <u>TACTICAL OBSERVATIONS</u>---

1. Referring to Section I, unusual risks were encountered in connection with the protection of the command post particularly while it was located at Sinemi Village. This latter location was admirable from the standpoint of ease of communication and control but there was a constant threat that bodies of the enemy might break through the swampy area between the Urbana and Warren Forces and attempt to disrupt our command system by a raid on the command post. As all troops in any condition to fight were required at the front, none could be spared for command post defense. Occasionally small bodies of exhausted troops were encamped in this area and part of them used for this duty although little real dependence was placed upon their effectiveness. The necessarily scattered installations of the command post, together with the jungle growth of the locality, opened up grave possibilities of creating great confusion and disruption if only a few of the enemy penetrated to the command post area particularly during the hours of darkness. However, a careful plan of defense was evolved, including organization of the ground; guards were furnished in accordance with this plan only at night. The personnel required necessarily came from officers and men already performing full time duties in the various headquarters sections. Fortunately no actual test occurred which indicated the effectiveness with which the plan could have been executed but it is seriously doubted whether any system of command post defense so organized would have been completely satisfactory even against a few really determined men. It is believed that this problem of command post defense can be solved only by the detailing of at least an organized defense platoon to this duty, otherwise there is always the possibility of a disaster.

2. Due to the fact that communication with both the Warren and Urbana Forces was definitely limited to the tracks mentioned in the general terrain study there never was any particular difficulty encountered in locating a straggler line. However, it must be pointed out that such a straggler line was practically useless. While it prevented personnel from entering the rear areas it could not be effective in keeping them on the front lines. The peculiar difficulties of supply and communication which required the use of many officers and men on this work, the elimination of identifying insignia and the ease with which individuals could lose themselves either voluntarily or involuntarily in the dense jungle growth led to a very definite and widespread dissipation of strength in the front lines. This whole condition was accentuated by a lack of appreciation of the necessity for utilizing the chain of command. The necessary discipline which would secure unhesitating obedience to orders and which would insure mutual trust and confidence in each other and in the unit was often lacking. There can be no doubt that particularly for jungle warfare identifying insignia, including company insignia, is necessary. Great emphasis must be placed upon the understanding of the use of the chain of command and disciplinary drills must be emphasized to insure unhesitating obedience to orders and to insure the feeling on everyone's part that each person in the unit can be depended upon to stand by each of the others whatever the surrounding conditions.

3. No difficulty was experienced in collecting and disposing of prisoners of war due largely to the fact that there were so few of them taken.

Prisoners of War in Buna Village

4. The personnel limitations placed on the American Forces in the Buna Area precluded the presence of a full complement of military police; in fact, only one officer and eight men were available for the collection and disposition of stragglers and prisoners of war.

Prisoner of War Cage

III. SYNOPTIC ACCOUNT OF THE CAMPAIGN---

Due to the almost impassable swamps which limited the American advance to corridors, the early stages of the campaign were conducted on the basis of combat team action and little attention was given to G-1 or AG functions for the force as a whole until early in December. With the arrival of one officer and one enlisted man from the I Corps, assisted by one officer and one enlisted man from the 32d Division, these functions were undertaken commencing December 12, 1942. Later the officer and enlisted man from the 32d Division were replaced by one officer, one warrant officer, and four enlisted men better qualified. Following are some of the more important problems to which thought need be given to insure their solution in future operations:

1. A number of officers were found to be ineffective during the campaign for other than physical reasons. Authority was secured for turning them over to the Advanced Base, USASOS, for disposition. This disposition involved no penalties for their ineffectiveness at the front. Only after the conclusion of the campaign was it determined that their cases could not be disposed of properly without resort to reclassification proceedings. Allowing these officers to return to places of comparative safety without immediate rather than uncertain and delayed penalties attached was an encouragement to poor performance of duty.

2. In action it is occasionally desirable that battle field promotions be made. Authority to do this did not exist in this campaign.

3. Authority did not exist to transfer officers and men within the Buna Forces. This operated to a marked degree as a hindrance to sound tactical organization.

4. Toward the end of the campaign, the 126th Infantry and, to a lesser degree, the 127th and 128th Infantry Regiments were reduced to practical ineffectiveness by personnel losses. As an illustration of the extent of this attrition, the following figures on the strengths of the various units of the 2nd Battalion, 126th Infantry, on three different dates, will prove interesting. This battalion saw some very heavy fighting and in addition had numerous malaria casualties. Without replacements, it can be seen how rapidly this organization went down.

2ND BATTALION, 126TH INFANTRY

	Dec. 2, 1942		Dec. 19, 1942		Jan. 5, 1943	
	Off.	EM	Off.	EM	Off.	EM
HQ CO	4	96	4	72	2	44
CO E	4	136	1	40		28
CO F	3	105	1	35	1	31
CO G	3	127	2	64	1	5
CO H	4	104	1	61		35
MED DET	1	17	1	11	1	11
TOTAL	19	585	10	283	5	154

No trained personnel replacements were made available to the Commanding General, Buna Forces, to replace these losses—in fact, no replacements as distinguished from casuals were known to be available in Australia. The 3rd Battalion of this regiment, which was under Australian command in the Sanananda Area, suffered even greater losses in strength. With an initial combat strength of 1199 officers and men, at the start of the campaign, it was reduced by January 9, 1943, to an effective strength of 90. While it was true that large numbers of officers and men, pertaining to the organizations of the Buna Forces, were in Port Moresby marked fit for duty they were really convalescents and would have been casualties within a few days if they had been returned to duty in the combat area. (See Annex #4, Inclosure E.)

5. If the campaign had continued longer, the problem of pay might have arisen. As it was there was absolutely nothing to spend money on in the area and no means of sending money home so there was no particular desire on the part of any of the personnel to be paid. It is doubted even if the campaign had lasted longer as to whether any large numbers would have cared to be paid with the resultant necessity of carrying this money around personally.

6. No particular difficulty was encountered in connection with the procurement of the necessary data as a basis for citations nor was there any particular delay in the approval of Silver Star citations. However, much of the effectiveness of these awards was lost due to the lack of the necessary medals and ribbons which should be available for immediate distribution. Unavoidable delay occurred due to the necessity of forwarding Distinguished Service Cross recommendations to higher headquarters.

7. Little opportunity existed for recreational and welfare work. The outstanding exception was the work of the Red Cross in distributing Christmas presents to each officer and enlisted man. The Red Cross undertook to send Christmas EFM messages from men at the front and in many cases also paid for them with the understand-

ing that this expense was to be taken care of by the individuals concerned at some later date. Unit chaplains were able to hold small services in areas behind the front lines.

8. Trained postal men were not provided to handle the mail of the Buna Forces. This resulted in poor service and in sending forward many items such as old magazines and newspapers that merely burdened down an already taxed communication system. Initially poor, there was a gradual improvement in the handling of first class mail.

9. Considerable difficulty was encountered in compiling accurate strength reports. Too much use was made of the telephone for this purpose by all concerned in the initial stages of the campaign.

10. During the first lull in the campaign immediately following the capture of Buna Mission, the personnel officers of the three infantry regiments were ordered to make a complete check of the status of all personnel of the 32d Division who had landed in New Guinea. This check was completed prior to January 25, 1943.

11. The collection and disposition of prisoners of war did not constitute a problem as so few were taken and these were easily disposed of by evacuating them immediately to Port Moresby. It was necessary to construct only a small prisoner of war inclosure, a few miles from the air strip.

12. Adequate provision was not made initially for graves registration and this condition persisted through the campaign. Too few personnel were assigned and too little supervision was given.

IV. SUMMARY OF LESSONS LEARNED----

1. To insure adequate control and the proper functioning of the chain of command and to minimize straggling, officers and men must be immediately identifiable as to rank and organization from some appreciable distance. Organizational identification for enlisted men should include the company designations.

2. Great emphasis must be placed upon the chain of command.

3. The traditional aids for the development and maintenance of discipline and promoting unit pride need more exacting emphasis. The goal must be a unit wherein individuals have mutual trust in each other's soldierly qualities and the utmost confidence in the ability of the unit to stick together under any circumstance and perform the task assigned.

4. Authority should exist for the transfer of any individual within a task force.

5. Authority should exist to transfer officers lacking in combat ability from units in combat to the Services of Supply for further reassignment. Reclassification proceedings should be instituted and carried through to completion without delay.

6. Authority to make battle field promotions in most exceptional cases in the lower commissioned grades should be granted a general officer.

7. A replacement center with trained replacement personnel should be available in the combat zone from the start of a campaign. When patients are discharged from hospitals serving combat troops, they should not be carried on a duty status but should be sent to a replacement center until they have been sufficiently recovered and hardened for full duty at the front.

8. A graves registration unit large enough to perform its duties properly and qualified postal personnel should be assigned from the start of a campaign.

9. Military police should be made available for the collection and disposition of stragglers and prisoners of war.

10. A defense platoon or other appropriate unit should be provided for the protection of any headquarters higher than that of the regiment.

11. Cemeteries should not be located in places frequently passed by combat troops.

12. The use of the telephone for routine administration must be definitely discouraged from the beginning of a campaign. Necessary conversations on administrative matters must be of a telegraphic brevity. Messenger service and telegraph facilities should be substituted wherever possible.

Appendix--Continued.

ANNEX #2
G-2 Report

GENERAL:

The Buna Campaign has been called "A Leavenworth Nightmare". Yet, it promulgated no new concept of G-2 operation but, on the contrary, indicated that our standard G-2 procedure is adequate for warfare in this theatre.

Failures were in execution, not in the fundamentals of standard training and operation. Thus, the cardinal G-2 conclusion to be drawn from the Buna Campaign is that our training program is satisfactory but must be **greatly** intensified. Training must be **made** more thorough, more **realistic**. For instance, a great deal of training in scouting and patrolling should be conducted at night; patrols should be **trained** to infiltrate through enemy outposts and move on objectives deep within the enemy position.

LESSONS:

These lessons are presented with a warning that they are deliberate attempts to ferret out weaknesses in our operation. There were many instances of brave and resourceful action although, as a general rule, intelligence work was poor in execution.

I. INTELLIGENCE TRAINING:

a. Scouting and Patrolling.

The first thing noted on arrival in the Buna Combat Zone was the paucity of information on hand concerning enemy-held terrain and enemy dispositions.

All available maps were inaccurate. Aerial photos, though requested, were not forthcoming to the scales and in the quantities needed; therefore, patrolling was the only recourse--patrolling which would have obtained needed information on both enemy-held terrain and enemy dispositions. Yet, no reasonable effort was being made to initiate patrolling. This was immediately corrected; however, throughout the campaign, front line commanders had to be prodded continually into maintaining adequate reconnaissance patrols.

Once patrolling was initiated, it was found that with few exceptions our patrols were neither determined, aggressive nor resourceful. They were consistent in their over-estimate of enemy strength and prowess (See "Propaganda" below). This led to "hiding out" and "fairy stories".

A typical example can be found in the actions of the first four patrols sent out. These patrols were given a mission to report on the terrain and enemy dispositions between Gerua Gardens and Giropa Point. They were instructed to move to the sea unless actually forced back by the enemy. If necessary, they were to stay out three days.

The first three patrols remained out less than 24 hours, although they reported no enemy encountered. Their reports were useless. Their information consisted mainly of "fairy stories".

The fourth patrol, before it was sent out, was given a discussion on the shortcomings of the three previous patrols. The discussion was concluded with a resume of "A Message to Garcia". This fourth patrol stayed out two days and on its return presented satisfactory results.

Had the men of the command been instilled with the resolute confidence that comes from severe, realistic training, the problems of scouting and patrolling would have been much less difficult.

Enemy patrols showed a commendable degree of training in the use of cover, silence, fire control, camouflage, and patience -- the ability to lie motionless for hours at a time in order to achieve their missions.

The best example of excellent enemy patrolling was the four man patrol located in the Command Post of the 127th Infantry. Two members of the patrol were killed but during the night the remaining two members stayed in the area and, among other things, buried their dead undetected.

The quantity and accuracy of intelligence produced by enemy reconnaissance patrols are not known, but one captured faulty estimate (See Enemy Intelligence, paragraph II a, below) would indicate that enemy patrols were not uniformly competent and successful.

b. <u>Message Writing</u>.

Message writing as a whole was not satisfactory either by officers or enlisted men. Time, place and direction of movement were the fundamental elements most frequently overlooked.

Examples are too numerous to mention, but the importance of accurate message writing must be further emphasized in future training.

c. <u>Map and Aerial Photo Reading</u>.

In jungle combat, map orientation is extremely difficult because of observation limitations and lack of landmarks. Further, accurate maps are rare if existing at all. (See "Map Procurement" under "Staff Work" below). The use of large scale aerial photographs and photo maps is a logical solution to this map problem which, in turn, means that troops must be schooled in the interpretation of aerial photographs, and the use of photo maps.

II. STAFF WORK.

a. Organization.

Despite the teachings of our schools and maneuver critiques, upon the arrival of the I Corps Staff in the Buna area, the 32d Division G-2 Section was not organized for continuous twenty-four hour operation; it had no intelligence plan; and had issued no intelligence instructions to troops. Energetic direction of intelligence efforts was lacking. As a result the situation map was, for all practical purposes, blank; and the division estimate of enemy strength in the sector east of the Girua River was 300, whereas the actual enemy strength was about 2200. This estimate was based on guesswork. It did not take into account known factors.

The lesson learned here was the value of proper organization as taught in our schools.

The merger of the skeletonized Corps G-2 Section with the Division G-2 Section was successful because all G-2 personnel had been given standardized training. Thus, one of the first lessons learned during the campaign was the advantage of standardized training.

For Intelligence staff work in echelons below corps and division, see "Utilization of Intelligence Personnel" below.

Enemy intelligence was not infallible. For example, a captured G-2 estimate, dated during the latter stages of the campaign, estimated the Allied strength at 1,200 whereas our actual strength (including Services of Supply) was about 6,000.

b. Utilization of Intelligence Personnel.

In echelons below corps and division, there was a marked tendency to use intelligence staff officers for anything from replacements to messengers. In some units it was necessary to convert staff officers to combat commanders because of the high casualty rate among the latter, but this should be avoided if possible.

Further, in many units intelligence platoons were used as infantry replacements. This practice is understandable in the light of the paucity of replacements and the high casualty rate, but, as in the case of intelligence officers, it should be avoided if possible.

c. Map and Aerial Photo Procurement.

Several months after the completion of the campaign, the Corps Commander learned for the first time that excellent large-scale aerial photos had been taken of the combat zone BEFORE the campaign was well started. Throughout the entire campaign, the I Corps continuously requested large scale aerial photos of the area. Few of the requests were filled and never in sufficient number to meet front line requirements. Had these maps been available casualties suffered by certain patrols would have been unnecessary.

Certainly, one of the cardinal lessons of the campaign is the need for a liaison between the ground forces and the air forces which will insure the taking, printing and distribution in quantity of large scale aerial photos.

Enemy maps, captured during the campaign, were copies of the small scale maps used by the Allies; none captured were as good as the 4" = 1 mile map used by Buna Force during the later stages of the campaign.

    d. Aerial Observation.

Aerial Observation during the campaign was from two sources: (1) a Wirraway squadron based at Dobodura and attached to the ground forces, and (2) combat missions flown from Port Moresby.

The fearless and consistently fine work of the Wirraways was extremely helpful. The missions from Port Moresby were less effective. The reasons are obvious. The Wirraway observers were thoroughly familiar with the terrain, were personally briefed by ground force officials who knew what information was important and why, and were flown in a manner by which the specific information they were after could be best obtained. Personnel flying combat missions from Port Moresby were not thoroughly familiar with the terrain (as is verified by their mistakes in the location of target areas), did not have the advantage of being personally briefed by ground force officials, and made their observations incident to bombing or strafing runs which are not necessarily satisfactory for the accomplishment of a specific observation mission.

The conclusion to be drawn is that observation squadrons or a ground-air support control should be under the command of the ground force commander.

    III. CAVALRY.

The terrain of the Buna Combat Zone precluded the employment of cavalry mounted (horse or mechanized). During the campaign there was no division reconnaissance troop in the area; however, one could have been used to advantage in dismounted reconnaissance.

Since the terrain of the Buna Combat Zone is not unlike that in areas of future operations in this theatre, it follows that division reconnaissance troops should be trained in dismounted scouting and patrolling and in dismounted combat to include attack and delaying action.

    IV. THE ENEMY.

        a. Interrogation and Translation.

For the interrogation of prisoners and the translation of captured documents, the Corps (Buna Force) G-2 Section had one language officer and three Nisei soldiers (second generation American Japanese). Below Buna Force Headquarters, each regimental headquarters had one Nisei.

Throughout the campaign these American Japanese soldiers were completely loyal, cheerful and competent. Their work, without exception, was excellent. (They had been trained at Camp Savage, Minn.) They were never allowed forward of regimental command posts, for had they been captured they undoubtedly would have been tortured.

Few of the Japanese prisoners taken during the campaign had identification tags. They would state that their tags had been lost, but during subsequent interrogation disclose their conviction that if it were announced that they were prisoners their families back in Japan would suffer. Thus prisoners did not like to disclose their real names.

Those identifications tags taken were not uniform. Some were wooden and others were rusted tin. Some prisoners maintained Japanese soldiers had to buy their own tags. It was not possible to determine whether or not identification tags are articles of issue in the Japanese army.

Without exception prisoners stated they had received no training covering their conduct if they were captured. Their code requires death rather than capture; therefore, the Japanese Army is neither in a position to recognize the possibility of a member becoming a prisoner nor to instruct him as to his conduct upon capture.

As a rule, prisoners talked freely but were disposed to be very technical when answering questions. For example, when asked the "military" strength of an area they would give their honest estimate but would NOT mention the presence of Marine units in the same area. Further, prisoners seemed to be generally truthful. A check was maintained by asking questions the answers to which were already known. On one occasion, a prisoner gave the location of an enemy supply dump near Giropa Point. This area was given the artillery as a suitable target. During the following concentration, a Wirraway observer witnessed the destruction of five enemy trucks and extensive damage to the hitherto hidden dump.

During the Buna Campaign, a great deal of information was gained from captured documents and diaries. Some of it is included in "Enemy Morale" and "What the Japanese Thought of Us", below.

The important interrogation lesson of the campaign is that full interrogation should be conducted at the command post of the force commander in the combat area for the following reasons:

(1) The best time to question prisoners according to the experience of our interrogators was between ten hours and one day after capture, when the prisoners were calming down from fear of torture and execution but before they had become "cocky" and had prepared a story.

(2) Little information of value was secured at regimental command posts.

(3) If full interrogation is not conducted at the force command post, and prisoners are hurried to a language center beyond the combat area, information would seldom be received by the front line troops in time to be of value.

(4) Adequate supervision by language officers of the work of language personnel is available at command posts of divisions and higher units, this is not true in the case of lower units.

Full interrogation should be made at the highest headquarters in the combat area, brief interrogation being made at intervening headquarters from divisions up. Therefore, except for detached combat teams it is believed that language personnel should not be employed forward of division command posts except for special missions, such as broadcasting appeals to surrender to hopelessly isolated enemy troops.

b. **Enemy Morale.**

Both statements of prisoners and captured documents indicated that: (1) Japanese patriotism and religion are synonymous; (2) Japanese soldiers are more emotional than generally thought; and, (3) Japanese morale will break.

The following statements, translated from diaries correlated with the course of campaign, speak for themselves:

"The morale of the troops is good because we feel reinforcements will come".

- 0 -

"Received word of praise from the Emperor today. We will hold out until the last".

- 0 -

"Warriors . . . must think of the example of Ko Yo Shi".

- 0 -

"Our troops do not come. Even though they do come they are driven away by enemy planes. Every day my comrades die one by one and our provisions disappear".

- 0 -

"We are now in a delaying holding action. The amount of provisions is small and there is no chance of replenishing ammunition. But we have bullets of flesh. No matter what comes we are not afraid. If they come, let them come, even though there be 1000. We will not be surprised. We have the aid of Heaven. We are the warriors of Yamamoto."

- 0 -

"How I wish we could change to the offensive. Human beings must die once. It is only natural instinct to want to live; but only those with military spirit can cast that away".

- o -

"There are some who are completely deteriorating spiritually."

- o -

"Today is finally the one year anniversary of the war. We should have a ceremony . . .".

- o -

"It is regrettable that there are many rumors going around about the battle situation".

- o -

"Mess gear is gone because of the terrific mortar fire. We can't eat today. Everyone is depressed. Nothing we can do".

- o -

"It is only fate that I am alive today. This may be the place where I will meet my death. I will fight to the last".

- o -

"Morale is low. Reinforcements do not come".

- o -

"With the dawn the enemy start shooting all over. All I can do is shed tears of resentment. Now we are waiting only for death. The news that reinforcements had come turned out to be a rumor. All day we stay in the bunkers. We are filled with vexation. Comrades are you going to stand by and watch us die. Even the invincible Imperial Army is at a loss. Can't anything be done? Please God".

- o -

"Night falls. Thought we saw two enemy scouts. It turned out to be a bird and a rat. A runner came and told of guards becoming completely afraid of the enemy and running back as a shot was fired. I said that was unbecoming of a Japanese soldier who had the great work of establishing peace in the Far East".

- o -

"It is certainly lamentable when everyone runs off

and not a single person remains to take care of things. Can these be called soldiers of Japan?"

- o -

"This is a deplorable state of affairs for the Imperial Army".

- o -

"I pray with the charm of the clan diety in hand".

- o -

According to prisoners of war and captured documents, the enemy feared our mortars first, our artillery second and our aerial strafing and bombing third. During the early stages of the campaign, the enemy reflected his lessons that the American soldier is not formidable. This point is further discussed in "Propaganda" below; however, the following extracts from Japanese diaries draw some rather interesting conclusions. The extracts are listed chronologically with the progress of the battle:

"The enemy has received almost no training. Even though we fire a shot they present a large portion of their body and look around. Their movements are very slow. At this rate they cannot make a night attack".

- o -

"The enemy has been repulsed by our keen-eyed snipers. In the jungle it seems they fire at any sound due to illusion. From sundown until about 10 P.M. they fire light machine guns and throw hand grenades recklessly".

- o -

"They hit coconuts that are fifteen meters from us. There are some low shots but most of them are high. They do not look out and determine their targets from the jungle. They are in the jungle firing as long as their ammunition lasts. Maybe they get more money for firing so many rounds".

- o -

"The enemy is using ammunition wildly. I wish the main force would hurry and come".

- o -

"The enemy has become considerably more accurate in firing".

- o -

"Enemy approached to about 50 meters. Difficult to distinguish their forms in the jungle. Can't see their figures".

- o -

"The nature of the enemy is superior and they excel in firing technique. Their tactics are to neutralize our positions with fire power, approach our positions under concentrated mortar fire. Furthermore, it seems that in firing they are using tree tops. During daytime mess, if smoke is discovered we will receive mortar fire".

- o -

"From today's mortar fire the third platoon received great damage."

- o -

"Headquarters is a pitiful sight due to artillery firing".

- o -

"Carried in one coconut tree and filled in all of the shelter. Now we are safe from mortar fire".

- o -

"Artillery raking the area. We cannot hold out much longer".

- o -

"Our nerves are strained, there is a lack of sleep due to the continuous night shelling".

- o -

"Enemy planes unbearable today".

- o -

"The enemy scouts which have been bothering us all night quit about two hours before dawn. The night strain has passed".

- o -

"Enemy scouts appear everywhere and attack shooting automatic rifles".

V. PROPAGANDA.

At the outset of the campaign our troops were entirely too impressed with the prowess of the Japanese soldier. To them, thanks to efficient enemy propaganda and the failure of Allied counter-propaganda, the Japanese soldier was a super-human beast who could take anything and give back more. Throughout the campaign it was necessary for all officers, repeatedly to point out to our troops the punishment they were giving the enemy.

On the other hand, the enemy were thoroughly schooled

to believe the American soldier was to be taken lightly, particularly in individual combat. While our troops were continually expecting the worst, the Japanese were surprised and unprepared for our determined offensive.

During the early stages of the campaign, Allied propaganda leaflets were dropped in the enemy positions. Statements by prisoners of war agree that the leaflets, particularly those which were poorly written, had no effect on breaking down Japanese morale. All of these leaflets dealt with the broad war picture; however, prisoners thought that had leaflets dealt directly with the situation at Buna they would have been more effective. Buna Force G-2 Section prepared such a leaflet but, as far as is known, it was not used.

Public address system surrender broadcasts to isolated groups of enemy were not used during the campaign because transportation restrictions precluded the dispatch of the necessary equipment to the combat area.

Appendix--Continued.

ANNEX #3
G-3 Report

I. GENERAL

No new principles of warfare were discovered during the Buna Campaign. The nature of the terrain and the disposition of the enemy necessitated some novel applications of well known principles. However, a consideration of the successes and failures encountered during the campaign will be valuable in training and planning for any future operations against the Japanese in similar positions. The illustrative examples given do not by any means, of course, exhaust the possibilities but it is felt that they give a useful cross-section of the action. In studying them, however, it must be remembered that, although failures may be stressed for the lessons involved, the American forces fought through to a victorious conclusion of the campaign.

II. TERRAIN

1. The general terrain influenced the fighting in many ways. The fact that the Japanese occupied all the high ground, had his flanks and rear resting on water and his front facing a series of swamps rendered anything but frontal attacks up well defined corridors the exception rather than the rule. It made the adoption of the penetration almost mandatory.

2. The unhealthy climate and terrain conditions under which our troops operated seriously affected the physical and mental health of the command. Men were evacuated for malaria or dysentery in numbers almost equal to the casualties from gun shot wounds. The psychological factors resulting from the terrain were also tremendously important. After a man had lain for days in a wet slit trench, or in the swamp his physical stamina was reduced materially. This reduction served to make him extremely nervous and to attribute to the unfamiliar noises of the jungle, spectres of Japanese activities. These reactions preyed on his mind until he was reduced often to a pitifully abject state, incapable of aggressive action. When removed from these conditions, properly fed and clothed he soon recovered his composure and regained his equanimity.

3. The nature of the terrain vitally affected the location of command posts. Distances were measured in terms of time rather than in terms of miles. The effective range of small arms fire (Japanese artillery fire was very rare) was usually so short and the vegetation so thick that command posts could be located much further forward than is normally the case. In one instance a regimental command post was within two hundred yards of one section of the line. Command posts had to be located close to the lines in order to permit the necessary staff visits without undue delay in moving forward. No observation posts were available from which local commanders could witness the action of their troops--only reports or personal visits to the front line would suffice to give the required information.

4. The difficulties presented by the terrain to the movement of units prevented the use of any general mobile reserve. A swamp between the Urbana and Warren Fronts necessitated a difficult two day march to move from one to the other. The Japanese on the other hand had a track behind their entire front, along which they operated motor vehicles. To be useful, a reserve had to be located close to the front which in effect made it only a local reserve.

5. The thick vegetation, providing cover and concealment for both attacker and defender, caused all fighting to be at close quarters. Our troops could not fight as units, but rather as individuals or in twos and threes. The vegetation prevented our troops from locating enemy positions until they stumbled on them. This precluded at times the use of artillery and mortar fire unless units were temporarily withdrawn. As a result many of our final assaults were made without benefit of supporting fire, a costly venture.

6. The terrain affected supply in that everything had to be carried and often by soldiers withdrawn from the front lines. This in turn affected operations. Every move that was made was dependent on the supply line. Less advantageous lines of action were sometimes adopted due to supply conditions.

III. LESSONS

    A. Operations.

        1. Japanese Defense

While a description of the Japanese defensive position is contained in the main body of this report, there are important G-3 lessons to be derived from a consideration of certain aspects of their defensive system. They had built bunkers with connecting trenches on all the high ground which forced any attacking force to advance frontally along rather narrow corridors of dry ground or through almost impassable swamps. The heavy jungle growth and kunai grass provided excellent natural concealment and the Japanese made clever use of them to camouflage their positions. They did not clear fields of fire but depended on close observation by snipers in trees to direct the fire of their automatic weapons.

The Japanese launched few counterattacks. In the last stages of the campaign large Japanese patrols occasionally attacked from the swamps in our rear area.

The policy of the Japanese seemed to be to sleep quite a bit during the day and work at night. This was in contrast to the American tendency to sleep at night and stay awake all day.

The Japanese were very economical in the expenditure of ammunition. The automatic weapon was fired with short bursts and only when a target presented itself. They always hesitated to deliver fire that might disclose their position. Generally they would fire only when being actively attacked or when our fire would prevent our locating the origin of the Japanese fire. For these reasons when our troops exposed themselves the Japanese would often be content to hold their fire. This practice would lead casual observers to believe that few if any Japanese were present in areas where in fact they might be concentrated in force.

Frequently the enemy would allow a large part of our attacking force to go by his concealed positions, and then open up with automatic weapons and grenades. This procedure proved disconcerting to our troops.

The Japanese would seldom surrender. When the plight of a unit became hopeless, instructions would evidently be issued for the survivors to try to escape individually or in small groups.

2. American Tactics

The Japanese position prevented any large scale envelopment. Since all of the easier avenues of approach were protected by bunkers it was generally necessary to attack through swamp which the Japanese considered impossible for our troops to use or across unfordable streams. Successive coordinated attacks all along the lines on both fronts were launched to discover and exploit soft spots or in any event to accomplish a break-through at some point. Wherever the Japanese perimeter was pierced the plan was to push more troops into the breach to carve out a corridor to the sea, thus splitting the enemy position into segments. Although, as has been pointed out, the use of reserves was limited by the terrain and the number of troops available, this plan proved highly successful when followed with determination.

The fighting frequently resolved itself into distinct small engagements to capture individual bunkers—a very difficult operation since in vulnerable positions the bunkers were so thick and so arranged in depth that flanking movements were almost impossible. This would indicate the desirability of training teams organized for this particular job with each member drilled in a specific set of duties. It must be realized that much of the thinking will have to be done before bullets start snapping on all sides and a dangerous enemy is waiting only a few yards away. During this campaign the circumstances were such that no particular method of attack could be generally adopted and tested in battle. Since our hand grenade was not powerful enough for use against bunkers all leaders constantly wished for some form of rifle grenade or "knee" mortar so that a powerful projectile could be fired with a relatively low trajectory and explode on impact.* It is believed that there should be a bunker eliminating squad which should include two or three men armed with the appropriate weapon. There should also be two or three men whose special responsibility would be to get the snipers who are the watchers for the usual Japanese bunker defense group. Then there must be the assault troops who will make the final charge.

*See discussion of hand grenade and anti-tank rifle grenade in "Employment of Weapons" paragraph 3, this section, this Annex. There were many times when the direct fire of a 75-mm howitzer could have been used effectively if such weapons had been available. An Australian 25 pounder was used successfully at times at close range.

A distinct tendency for squad and platoon leaders to deploy their units too soon was observed. This resulted in a premature loss of control and a consequent halting of the attack. An ordinary line of skirmishers advancing through jungle terrain would in addition cause many individuals to become lost.

Orders should be brief and clear and objectives easy to understand. Complicated ideas cannot be remembered or even grasped in the heat of the fire fight.

An effort was made to use Bren gun carriers on the Warren Front with no success. The personnel in the carriers were shot from tree top positions and the carriers themselves lacked sufficient power and weight to cope with the type of bunker against which they were sent.

Tanks were exceedingly valuable where open terrain and the dryness of the ground made their employment possible. On December 18, American built light tanks operated by Australians attacked the Japanese positions at Cape Endaiadere. Followed closely by Australian infantry, they broke through the enemy bunker system. American infantry quickly poured in to occupy the ground gained. Several tanks were put out of action either by enemy fire* or the difficulties of the terrain and the Australian infantry took about fifty per cent casualties but the job was done. Later on the Sanananda track the tanks were not effective because their operation was limited by swamps and jungle to the track itself.

Japanese pompom captured on Old Strip.

After each attack it is important that a reorganization take place. One of the reasons that by December 2 American attacks had deteriorated into half-hearted and feeble gestures was the widespread mixing of units. The fact that time was pressing and hast was vital rendered the resting of units impossible and reorganization difficult. Intelligent and energetic efforts on the

* Japanese 13-mm anti-aircraft pompoms were effective when used against our light tanks.

part of battalion and company commanders can accomplish much, however, even when a unit cannot be moved into a rear rest area.

After an attack had moved through an area it was necessary to make a careful search for hidden Japanese. The enemy would hide in trees and in holes in the ground, and would not infrequently play dead among the bodies of his companions who had been killed. They would make false gestures of surrender. All of these deceptions were activated by a desire to avoid capture and to kill as many of our men as possible before they were themselves eliminated.

That constant and aggressive reconnaissance by leaders and by patrols is one of the most vital phases of successful battle operations was demonstrated vividly many times. The fact that the closeness of the jungle growth and the well-concealed enemy positions made this task very difficult only increased its importance. On the Sanananda track it was reported that there were only one machine gun and a few riflemen defending the area being attacked by the Australian 7th Division as well as by elements of the 126th Infantry and later by the 163d Infantry. Reconnaissance parties sent out were unable to determine the strength of the enemy. When the position was finally captured there were between 75 and 80 machine guns in the area and over 300 Japanese killed in the bunkers. On the Urbana Front several patrols were sent out to determine the extent and disposition of the Japanese in the "Triangle". Reports that were brought back varied from one to seven bunkers, but when the position was captured eighteen mutually supporting bunkers were found.

3. Employment of Weapons

a. *The Bayonet*: Although in isolated instances the bayonet may have been used as a weapon, in general it was found that it was not much employed. While this does not mean that it could not be used very profitably by well trained troops, it does seem to indicate that the bayonet has limited value in jungle terrain.

b. *The Hand Grenade*: The hand grenade was used frequently with excellent effect. It was found that heavily constructed Japanese bunkers were impervious to the explosive effects of our grenades but used against open trenches or groups of enemy in the open it was very effective. It was much superior to the Japanese hand grenade which was largely detonation with little fragmentation. When our grenades were reinforced by attaching blocks of TNT to them they were much more satisfactory against bunkers.

c. *The M-1 Rifle*: The M-1 rifle was a satisfactory weapon. While it was not as popular as the Thompson submachine gun and lacked the advantages of lightness and shortness possessed by the carbine, it was nevertheless successful when properly used. Because of its accuracy and power some leaders preferred it to any other shoulder weapon. Most leaders because of lightness and simplification of ammunition supply, looked forward to the issue of the new carbine.

d. *The Thompson Submachine gun*: The Thompson submachine gun was the most popular weapon among the soldiers in the campaign. They would usually pick up this weapon if found on the battlefield and abandon the M-1 rifle. While its weight is roughly equivalent to the M-1 rifle, its shortness and automatic fire power are important advantages in close terrain.

   e. **The M-9 Antitank Grenade**: This grenade was experimented with but it was found that it failed to detonate unless fired against a very hard object. It has been noted elsewhere in this report that a rifle grenade which could be fired with a low trajectory and which would explode on contact would seem to be very desirable.

   f. **The 37-mm Antitank Gun**: Initially the 37-mm gun was used only to a limited extent but when used with cannister in the Tarakena area it proved itself a very effective weapon to accompany infantry. Cannister from these guns would sweep the Japanese from their tree positions and direct fire of high explosive against bunkers was destructive.

   g. **The 81-mm Mortar**: The 81-mm mortar was probably the most effective weapons used during the campaign. When grouped in batteries of six or more and fired by forward observers they could place accurate and devastating fire on any part of the Japanese positions within range of the weapon. On the Sanananda Front mortar fire destroyed emplacements; however, on the Buna Front the use of cocoanut logs by the Japanese rendered the mortar shell less effective. The weight of this weapon and the weight of its ammunition are of course disadvantages that must be considered where they have to be manhandled for long distances.

   h. **The 60-mm Mortar**: In spite of inadequate training in the use of this weapon it proved very valuable in the hands of several organizations. Since these weapons went forward with the rifle companies the men carrying them were often exposed to enemy fire and as a result some mortars were abandoned. Naturally, the 60-mm mortar firing a smaller shell had less destructive effect than the 81-mm mortar.

   i. **Artillery**: The employment of artillery during this campaign is discussed in an artillery report which has been made an inclosure to this annex.

  B. Conduct of the Individual.

   1. **Fighting Technique of the Soldier**:

    a. **Use of Cover and Concealment**: As was to be expected the individual soldier without previous combat experience was excited and nervous when subjected to enemy fire. In spite of his natural desire to avoid being hit, however, he usually failed to make the best use of cover and concealment. Often soldiers who would advance with extreme timidity and lack of aggressiveness in an attack would at other times expose themselves with great carelessness within a few yards of the Japanese positions. For example, members of a unit on the spit of Buna Mission which had been pinned down by effective fire from Japanese bunkers a few yards away were found sitting in a group laughing and smoking within hand grenade range of the bunkers. It is not enough that the principles of using cover and concealment be taught--the application must be drilled into the soldier until it becomes automatic.

b. Fire Discipline and Control: Officers and non-commissioned officers generally failed to realize the importance of fire discipline and fire control. At certain times and places firing was wild and prolonged, at imaginary targets or no targets at all. At other times and places observed targets were not fired upon because of the disinclination of the individual soldier to draw enemy fire.

Examples of wild firing:

On January 4th our flank protection at Tarakena was attacked by a small force of Japanese from the swamp. The Americans opened fire blindly and in thirty minutes had exhausted their supply of ammunition. They then withdrew in disorder.

On December 28th when K Company of the 127th Infantry was ordered to advance by boat and cross the bridge from the island in Entrance Creek to Buna Mission the blind and uncontrolled firing by Americans was an important reason why the attack did not move forward as intended. It was obvious from the moment this spontaneous and irresponsible firing started that there would be no further progress until a reorganization had taken place.

Excitedly firing at noises during the night was a common fault and seriously restricted the use of patrols and other important movements after dark.

Machine gunners habitually fired long bursts of from twenty to thirty rounds at targets which at most would call for a slow rate of fire.

Examples of failure to fire at targets:

On December 2, General Eichelberger visited the American units held up on the outskirts of Buna Village. At one position the occupants stated they thought there were snipers in some of the trees to their front. When some of the General's group prepared to fire into these trees, strenuous objections were made on the ground that such action would draw enemy fire. Although these objections were disregarded, no enemy fire was received.

After the fall of Buna Mission small groups of Japs endeavored to escape by making their way through the swamps in the rear of the American lines. In at least two instances guards withheld fire in order to avoid being fired on themselves.

In both aspects of lack of fire discipline and control illustrated above the nervousness and fear of the individual soldier concerned as well as the inefficiency of certain small unit leaders were in considerable measure to blame. Observers, however, were convinced that most of this could be remedied by proper training in combat firing with emphasis on fire discipline rather than on volume of fire.

Much of the American firing was very inaccurate. Captured Japanese documents refer to the fact that American firing was usually too high, particularly during the earlier days of the fighting. Some captured trucks had hundreds of bullet holes in the bodies but retained air in unpunctured tires.*

Tires not punctured

2. Discipline.

There are various degrees of discipline to which troops may attain as a result of their native intelligence, willpower, and training. Some soldiers obey commands as long as they are closely supervised. Some will obey orders without close supervision. Some will carry out the principles learned during their training without specific orders. It is apparent that the better the discipline of a unit and its leader the less supervision is required by the higher commander to accomplish the desired goals. The shortcomings discussed under "Supervision and Inspection" then would have been eliminated if a high degree of discipline had existed in the ranks or in the lower echelons of command.

One reason for the poor discipline encountered was the habitual elimination of insignia of rank and military courtesy in the combat area. It is believed that insignia of rank should be worn, but that it should be made so that it will not reflect light or be recognizable more than a short distance away. Military courtesy should be continued insofar as the exigencies of the situation allow. As the commander of the Urbana Force stated: "Enlisted men usually remained in a reclining or sitting position when spoken to by officers even though out of sight of the enemy. Saluting was about as rare as snow in Papua. Military courtesy

* See G-2 Annex.

should be restricted in battle zones but not eliminated. During this campaign almost all semblance of military courtesy was eliminated and a loss of control was evident."

3. **Problems of Leadership**

a. <u>Supervision and Inspection</u>: Every phase of the Buna Campaign illustrated again and again the fact that after a leader has made his estimate of the situation and has issued his orders his job has just begun. One of the most glaring causes of failure among battalion and regimental commanders was their failure to supervise closely the execution of orders. The Commanding General of the Buna Force constantly sent staff officers to the scene of important activity and himself frequented the forward areas. It was found that where this supervision was lacking, orders, in many cases, would not be carried out.

Nothing of importance can be left to the individual inclination of the soldier. The taking of quinine, the care of insect bites, the maintenance of weapons, shaving and bathing, avoidance of sleeping on the ground are all subjects about which specific instructions must be issued and diligently enforced. Adequate training of troops makes this task easier, but detailed supervision is a responsibility that cannot be avoided by combat leaders under any circumstances.

Regimental and battalion commanders must supervise the evacuation and treatment of the sick and alleged sick. One of the pithiest statements made during the campaign was that a big hearted medical officer with a thermometer can cause defeat as quickly as Japanese bullets. Malaria was of course very prevalent since mosquito bars were scarce near the front line and there were indications that some men deliberately failed to take quinine or atabrine in order that they might be evacuated. Fevers were doubtless derived from various causes other than malaria. Brig. Gen. Martin (then Colonel) brilliantly commanded the 128th Infantry from December 3 until the end of the campaign although during a large part of that time he had a fever that would have caused the evacuation of a less determined man. The judgement of the medical officers in handling evacuation may have a decisive bearing on the outcome of a battle.

The energy displayed by the Japanese in digging in at every opportunity was in sharp contrast to the laziness and indifference of many of the small American units in constructing field fortifications. A glaring example was the 37-mm gun discovered by the Buna Force commander set up in an open space within 300 yards of Japanese bunkers near the junction of the New and Old Strips. It had no protection except the gun shield provided for the crew. Ration boxes were available and could have been filled with dirt and emplaced with an hour's work. Intelligent and aggressive supervision by company and battalion commanders should insure adequate local protection for our troops.

b. <u>Morale</u>: Well trained troops would be expected to behave better than hastily trained troops when first exposed to enemy fire. After the battle has been joined, however, there is no longer time to prepare soldiers for the emotional trials incident to war, but there are many things the leader can and must do to help his men.

Staff officers inspecting units at the front became convinced that officers were far too prone to sympathize with nervous and frightened soldiers. It is believed that such misguided sympathy was a strong contributing factor in causing straggling and failure to attack with determination. On the other hand, it was found that even under the worst conditions most men would respond to cheerfulness and humor on the part of leaders. In this connection visits of higher commanders to the front line noticeably increased the fighting spirit of the troops there.

Soldiers should be kept informed of the situation, not only to enable them to act intelligently but to encourage them. On one occasion the Commanding General of the Buna Force asked members of a unit, glumly waiting to go into action, whether they knew of certain American successes elsewhere. They did not; their officers had failed to pass on this information. When told about these American victories and the desperate plight of the Japanese, their spirits visibly rose and they later went into the fight with vastly more spirit than would otherwise have been the case.

Wherever possible, it is believed desirable to assign men in pairs for outpost duty, guard duty and scouting. The presence of even one other soldier, particularly at night, bolsters the spirits of a man tremendously.

The personal cleanliness of troops aside from its effect on the health of the command had an important bearing on its discipline and morale. Where a high state of discipline and morale exist troops will without instructions keep themselves as clean as the conditions under which they are living allow, and a corollary to this is that where cleanliness of person and equipment are enforced discipline and morale will thereby improve. Opportunities to shave and to bathe were few during this campaign. Yet in many cases where facilities were available or could be made available no effort was made to take advantage of the opportunity. When new leaders insisted upon shaving and bathing and proper care of clothing and equipment, the efficiency of the organizations visibly improved.

c. *General Conclusions about leadership*: Throughout all of the lessons discussed in this report, whether expressed or implied, the element of leadership is an important factor. Examples of defeated units becoming revitalized under vigorous leadership were numerous. In fact the whole campaign is a convincing demonstration that with a given unit—whether division, regiment, company, or platoon—vigorous and efficient leadership is the difference between success and failure. All commanders, in training and in battle, must ruthlessly weed out incompetent leaders, and energetically seek out new leaders in their units. Failure to be "hard boiled" in this respect will render a unit commander, otherwise capable, impotent to achieve the results desired.

The combat leader must use every means at his disposal to train his men properly before battle is joined, to bring his men into contact with the enemy in the best possible fighting trim and yet be tough minded enough to expend them unhesitatingly to achieve victory.

1 Incl.
  A - Field Artillery Report

Appendix—Continued.

Annex #3
Inclosure A
Field Artillery Report

The artillery present in the BUNA - SANANANDA area consisted of:

    1 Troop 25 pounder, 2/1 Field Regiment, Captain Manning

    1 Troop 25 pounder, 2/5 Field Regiment, Major Hall

    1 Troop 25 pounder, Captain Hansen

    1 Troop 3.7 (3 Howitzers), 1st Australian Mountain Battery, Major O'Hare

    1 Troop 4.5 Howitzer, 14th Field Regiment, Captain Stokes

    1 - 105-mm Howitzer of Battery A, 129th Field Artillery Battalion, Captain Kobs.

The Hansen troop was in the vicinity of Soputa supporting the Seventh Australian Division. Its firing in the Buna area was limited to a little harassing fire about the 10th and 12th of December.

The O'Hare troop ran out of ammunition about 26 December 1942 and took no further part in the battle.

In the early part of the campaign before the recapture of Kokoda, it was apparently thought that artillery could not be used. So there seems to have been little planning of its organization, installation, or ammunition supply.

About 16 November 1942, the O'Hare and Hall troops arrived at Oro Bay. Brigadier General Albert W. Waldron, 32d Division Artillery, and Lieutenant Colonel Melvin L. McCreary, with the aid of a captured Japanese barge and small boats, worked these pieces along the coast until finally about 22 November they were in position just off the coastal trail south of Cape Endaiadere. After the 3.7s had been landed near Embogo, the barge carrying two 25 pounders north from Oro Bay was sunk by enemy air action in the late afternoon with the loss of the guns and most of the troop equipment. The remaining two guns had to be taken down using improvised tools to permit transport by small boats.

On 25 November, the Manning troop was flown in to Dobodura and went into action near Ango.

On 13 November, one 105-mm howitzer of Battery A, 129th Field Artillery Battalion was taken down and together with one officer, the howitzer section of 8 men, one Australian tractor, and 25 rounds of ammunition, was flown from Brisbane to Port Moresby in a B-17. The other three pieces were flown from Brisbane to Moresby similarly. The move was completed about 22 November. Comment on loading the B-17 is that while the total weight is not excessive, the distribution of the load puts strain on structural members that are not designed to carry that much. The LB-30 airplane would have been better. One 105-mm howitzer was flown from Port Moresby to Dobodura on 26 November in three DC-3 transport planes loaded:

    Plane No. 1 - Howitzer and section equipment.

    Plane No. 2 - Tractor and howitzer squad.

    Plane No. 3 - 100 rounds 105-mm ammunition.

This piece went into position about 400 yards south of Ango and under the code name of "Dusty" remained there throughout the campaign.

About 20 December, one troop of four 4.5 howitzers (Australian) were flown in and emplaced south of the Warren front. This troop later furnished the direct support for the operations against Tarakena and Gerua.

The I Corps Artillery Officer and a detachment from the Headquarters Division Artillery, 32d Infantry Division including 5 officers and the communication platoon formed the Buna Force Artillery Headquarters. This group reported for duty on December 8 and 9, 1942.

About 14 December, it was necessary to form two advanced command posts, one to operate with each force. With this setup and a wire net with very long lines, it was possible to support the two widely separated forces with what amounted to less than a battalion of artillery.

Ground observation was very limited. Only small areas could be seen from trees generally in the infantry front lines. Air observation, thanks to virtual control of the air by our forces and the superb work of the Australian air observers using Wirraways, established numerous registered points in enemy territory and adjusted fire on many targets of opportunity.

Some air photos were available and were of assistance but lack of liaison with the air force prevented securing photos wanted. A fire control chart was developed from one photo (6-(Sch-51C) (Buna Sanananda Point Area) (27 November 1942) 15,000', 6" F.L.) and a 1/5000 scale strip Cape Endaiadere to Buna Mission taken December 10, 1942, was very helpful to forward observers.

Many times infantry were alarmed by their own artillery fire because they had never been fired over. They could not distinguish between their own and enemy artillery. At first, they wanted to drop back 300 yards or more before artillery was fired on a close-in objective. Later as they had more experience, they got closer to the bursts of their own artillery.

Ammunition supply by air and sea was controlled by priorities set up by Advanced New Guinea Forces. Because of limited transport to the combat area, artillery firing was frequently restricted to conserve ammunition. For details on ammunition supply, see the G-4 and Ordnance Annexes. Although the 105 howitzers were flown in by air and arrived at Port Moresby toward the end of November, ammunition for them was not available in any quantity until late in December. Guns are worthless without ammunition.

LESSONS LEARNED

1. Artillery of standard calibers can be used much more extensively in this theater than was originally supposed. The 105-mm howitzer can be air borne. In many situations, the guns can be brought in by sea or air but may not be able to move far from the landing area. This will more often be caused by supply difficulties than because the weapon itself can not be moved up. This indicates the need of artillery weapons of long range.

2. It is believed that the efficient artillery support was largely due to the excellent work of the forward observer. The Australian forward observer proved to be courageous and well trained. He was often ahead of his infantry.

3. Infantry must have had experience of their own artillery firing over their heads and as close in as safety regulations permit. Artillery must have the experience of firing close to their own infantry, so as to be impressed with the accuracy necessary.

4. Infantry must have impressed on them the necessity of attacking immediately after the artillery preparation lifts. There were many instances where all effect of the artillery fire was wasted because the enemy were allowed ample time to reorganize and recuperate from the shock of the artillery fire before the infantry was ready to advance.

5. In many instances, the nature and dispositions of the enemy resistance were not discovered until the infantry were in such close contact with the resistance that artillery and mortars could not be used. This was caused by a combination of the dense country in which the operations were staged and poor scouting and patrolling by the infantry.

6. Dense jungle foliage limits the effective radius of burst so that the neutralization of indefinitely located targets, "Machine guns in the vicinity of. . .", was not effective. Even accurately located targets required more than the amount of ammunition normally thought adequate.

7. The 105-mm howitzer with delayed fuze proved effective against bunkers and pill boxes constructed of cocoanut logs. The 3.7, the 25 pounder, and the 81-mm mortar were not entirely effective against this construction.

8. Harassing fire in areas known or suspected to be occupied by the enemy was very effective in destroying enemy morale. This was verified by prisoners and captured diaries. It must be noted, however, that the enemy in this situation occupied a very restricted area.

9. The enemy early discovered that we did not fire harassing fire close to our own troops and moved into these areas.

10. In this stabilized situation, the 81-mm mortar grouped into batteries and fired by artillery methods was tremendously effective. Seventeen mortars (one less than Tables of Basic Allowances for an infantry regiment) were used. Five hundred rounds of mortar ammunition were fired in one day on one occasion. This

is a 3½ ton supply item. The limited amount of ammunition that could be brought into the area directly determined the amount of artillery and mortars that could be used.

11. The following factors must be remembered in studying this campaign:

    a. The situation was stabilized.

    b. The area occupied by the enemy was small.

    c. Our force had air superiority. Much of the time we had definite control of the air.

    d. The enemy artillery in the Buna area was limited to five 75-mm naval guns which could be used as dual purpose guns. There were a few 37-mm guns and also some 20-mm guns which had been taken from Zeros. There were only a few heavy mortars.

Captured Japanese Naval Gun
on Old Strip

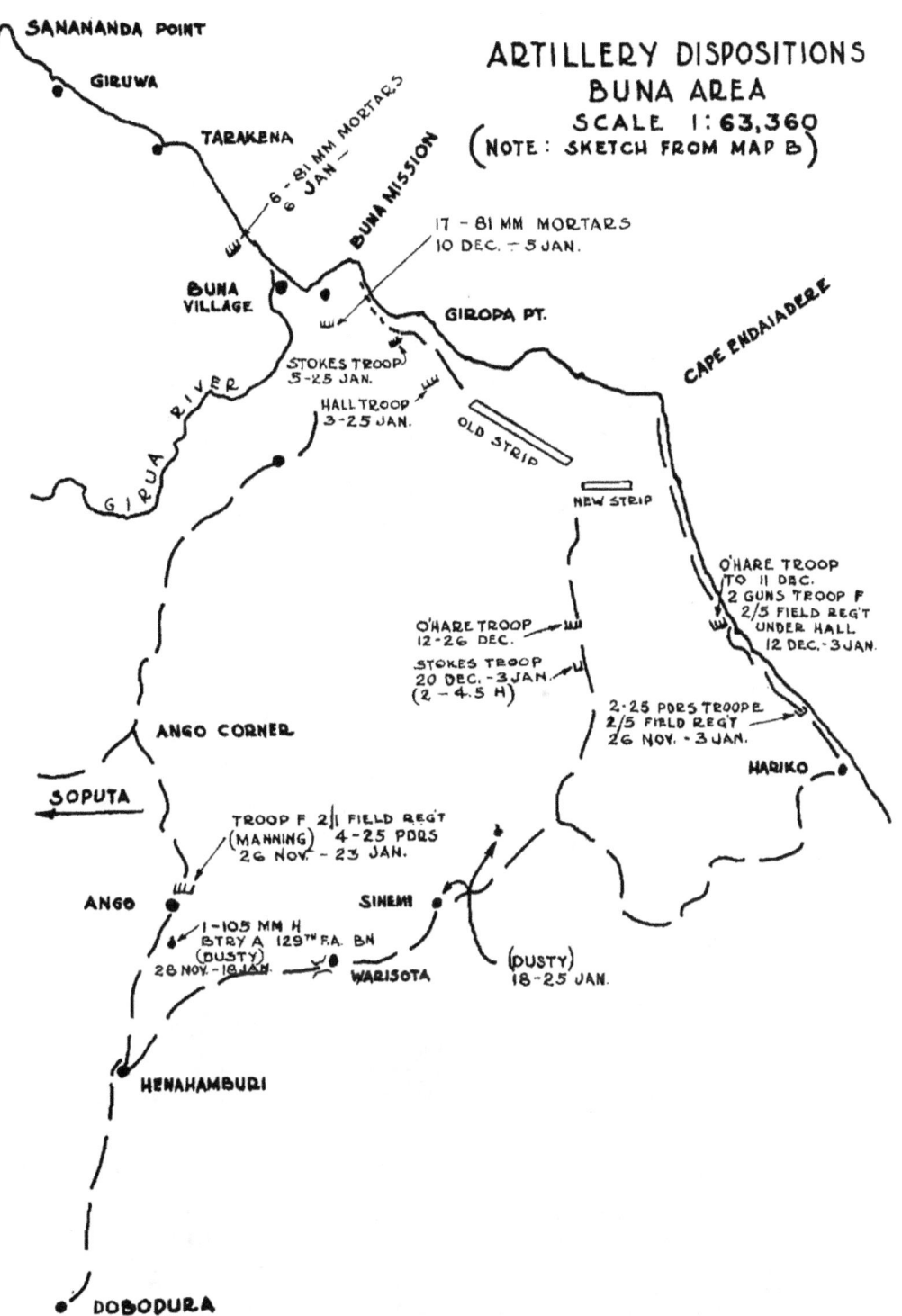

Appendix--Continued.

ANNEX #4
G-4 Report

1. SUPPLY:

Two modes of transportation were used to supply the Buna Forces, by air from Port Moresby to supply base at Dobodura, and by water from Oro Bay to Hariko. Prior to the fall of Buna, all troops of the Urbana Force (west flank) were supplied from the Dobodura base. Troops of the Warren Force (east flank) were supplied from the Hariko base. Requests for supply requirements by air were consolidated by the G-4 Section, Buna Force (US), and transmitted to Advanced Headquarters, New Guinea Forces, which in turn transmitted these requests to Headquarters, New Guinea Forces, Port Moresby, for delivery the following day. Safe-hand letters were sent daily to the Rear Echelon, 32d Division, in Port Moresby listing specific critical supply requirements which included the requests made on Advanced NGF noted above.

The rear echelon group was in constant liaison with NGF at Port Moresby and assisted materially in procuring air priorities to fill critical supply requirements for delivery to the Buna forces. The final decision on what supplies would be flown to the combat zone was made by NGF in Port Moresby. Due to the number of troops participating in the campaign and the numerous priorities requested, together with adverse flying conditions, deliveries by air were uncertain. The following quoted telegram from Advanced NGF in the combat zone to Headquarters, NGF, Port Moresby, needs no amplification other than that the commander in the combat zone is in the better position to determine supply requirements and priorities than is a rear echelon commander south of the Owen Stanley Range 103 miles away:

"ADV NGF TO RRD   IMPORTANT
NR 7 ORIG NR SD 261   13 JAN 43
TO NGF RPTD 7 AUST DIV 32 US DIV
FROM ADV NGF

COMD TO SEE. AIR PRIORITIES 14 JAN. NO CHANGE PRIORITIES ALREADY REQUESTED. MORE THAN 600 PATIENTS AWAITING EVACUATION FROM POP. OF 115000 POUNDS DELIVERED DOB TODAY 75000 WERE ENGR EQUIPMENT FOR FIGHTER STRIP AND NOT REQUESTED FROM THIS HQ. ROADS TO HARIKO SOPUTA AND ORO NOT REPEAT NOT YET TRAFFICABLE"

Supply requirements for the Warren Force were consolidated by the G-4 Section, transmitted to Advanced NGF, which in turn transmitted these requests to CO, supply base, Oro Bay, for delivery under cover of darkness. Supplies from Oro Bay were transported to the Hariko Base during active operations by small boats and barges normally between the hours of 11 PM and 4:30 AM. Movement of the bulk of these supplies from ship to shore was made by small barge and surf boats similar to those used as lifeboats on commercial liners. On numerous occasions supplies were lost due to high seas and swamping of boats and barges. The shortage of power boats and barges considerably handicapped the movement of supplies from ship to shore. On numerous occasions supply ships returned to Oro Bay only partially unloaded due to these handicaps. The Small Boat Section operating from Oro Bay was under control of the Navy (NOIC). Regardless of status of unloading, these boats would return to Oro Bay from Hariko at 4:30 AM in compliance with navy orders. During the closing days of the campaign this time limit was extended to 8:30 AM. It is believed that movement of supplies by water could have been accomplished more efficiently during daylight hours in view of the fact that air cover was always provided in the Buna area for air transport deliveries. If this air cover was adequate for these air transport movements, it would appear to have been sufficient protection for sea movements to a port about 11 air miles away.

Supplies were moved from the Dobodura and Hariko bases to regimental and similar unit dumps on jeeps and trailers under control of the supply base commanders. Native carriers supplemented jeeps and trailers when roads became impassable.

2. AMMUNITION:

Insofar as practicable and available, a level of approximately five units of fire, all calibers, was maintained in the Buna area. This ammunition was stocked in dumps at Dobodura and Hariko, with the Warren Force, Urbana Force, and field artillery batteries. Levels of ammunition with combat troops were based on daily reports of regimental ammunition officers and their requests for future operations. Shortages of 37mm cannister, 81mm mortar heavy and hand grenades required exacting control of deliveries to using troops. The supply of artillery ammunition was controlled by Advanced NGF.

3. HOSPITALIZATION AND EVACUATION:

The portable hospitals attached to each infantry battalion proved indispensable during this campaign. These hospitals were provided with outstanding surgeons and personnel. In emergencies, portable hospitals were equipped to care for patients for two or three days. Patients were evacuated from portable hospitals to the 2d Platoon, 2d Field Hospital, which was located near the supply base at Dobodura. Slightly wounded cases were evacuated by returning jeep supply vehicles. Seriously wounded cases (head, chest, abdomen and fractures) were evacuated by native carriers. Evacuations from the 2d Platoon, 2d Field Hospital, were made by air to Port Moresby. No evacuations were made by sea with the exception of a number of Japanese prisoners who were moved from the Tarakena-Buna-Sanananda areas during the closing days of the campaign. These were moved by barge to Oro Bay for trans-shipment to Milne Bay and Port Moresby.

4. ROADS:

Other than native trails, roads and tracks were practically nonexistent in the Buna area. Heavy rains and mud required constant engineer work to keep these trails open during the entire operation. At the close of the campaign, trails north and west of Ango, north of Sinemi to Cape Endaiadere, east of Borio to Oro Bay, and east of Sinemi to Hariko were impassable for motor vehicles. The 114th Engineer Battalion, 32d Division, was normally augmented by 400 natives to assist in road and bridge construction. However, at

Wounded were evacuated by native carriers

. . . and by jeeps

times when trails became impassable it was necessary to use all native labor in the Buna area to carry supplies and ammunition which seriously retarded road and trail improvement. Two general service engineer regiments could have been used continuously during this campaign on road and bridge construction with distinct advantage. The low flat swamplands of the Buna area were impossible to drain with the equipment available. These were converted into quagmires with water at times four and five feet deep following heavy rains. Many trails had to cross such areas.

5. TRANSPORTATION:

Quarter ton jeeps and trailers were the only type transportation used during the Buna campaign. The performance of these vehicles was superior. During the early stages of the campaign, the only means of getting these vehicles into the area was by air transport which is the principal reason why no other type vehicle was used. Due to mud and impassable roads, a request was submitted to the I Corps Rear Echelon, Port Moresby, to provide dual rear wheels and also oversize tires for vehicles in the Buna area. Both of these expedients greatly improved the performance of these vehicles in negotiating mud and swamplands. If it had been possible to fly them in, it is believed that the new 3/4 ton Dodge vehicle would have equaled or surpassed the performance of the jeep in the Buna area.

6. NATIVE LABOR:

Native labor was acquired, controlled and allotted by Advanced NGF. Allotment to the Buna Force was initially as follows:

```
 406   Engineer, 32d Division
 300   Dobodura Supply Base
 340   Hariko Supply Base
 400   Urbana Force
 160   Surgeon, 32d Division
1606
```

At times when roads became impassable, it was necessary to use all of these natives as carriers for supply purposes. During the closing days of the campaign, inclement weather prevented supply by air from Port Moresby which practically exhausted the supply level of rations and ammunition at the Dobodura Supply Base. For a period of a week, due to heavy rains and impassable roads for motor traffic, it was necessary to supply the entire 7th Australian Division and attached troops by a three-stage carrier line from Hariko to Soputa area. Every ablebodied native available to Advanced NGF was used for this purpose. Unless these natives had been available, supply of troops participating in this campaign would have been impossible without withdrawing hundreds of combat troops for supply purposes.

7. GENERAL REMARKS:

In order to provide against any contingency which might arise, an effort was made throughout the Buna Campaign to establish a minimum level of 30 days supply, all classes, in the Dobodura and Hariko supply bases. Due to the meager transportation facilities available, adverse weather conditions and immediate critical daily requirements, this objective was never attained. Only on one occasion, and then for rations alone, did the supply level at these two bases reach the figure of approximately 16 days. At the close of the campaign, many supplies were transshipped by water from Hariko to Giropa Point, Buna and Sanananda, all of which are in front of the coastal defense positions. Counterattack by the enemy in force in the Buna area would have seriously threatened and possibly eliminated supply of defending troops by water. Immediate priority should have been given to the construction of main and access supply roads from these areas to the seacoast. A minimum of two engineer general service regiments should have been dispatched to the Buna area for this purpose. In conclusion it might be stated that regardless of transportation difficulties encountered in this campaign, food, ammunition, clothing and essential critical needs were provided and delivered to participating troops.

G-4 SUMMARY OF LESSONS LEARNED DURING BUNA CAMPAIGN

1. Supply which is dependent solely on air transport for delivery requires detailed joint advanced planning by representatives of the task force commander, the air transport command, and advanced base serving the task force. These representatives must remain in constant and intimate contact during the entire campaign.

2. Supply by air requires the services of a trained unit to handle for the task force the supply requirements in rear areas from advanced base supply agencies to transport airplanes. This unit should consist of the following sections as a minimum:

    Headquarters Section
    Procurement Section
    Wrapping Section
    Loading and Dropping Section
    Transportation Section

3. Transport planes making deliveries to the task force in the combat zone must be unloaded with dispatch to eliminate danger of enemy bombing and strafing. This responsibility rests with the task force commander.

4. Supply which is dependent on small boats for delivery requires detailed joint advanced planning by representatives of the task force commander, advanced base commander, and commander of the boat section serving the task force. These representatives must remain in constant and intimate contact during the entire campaign. Experience in the Buna Campaign indicated that it is highly desirable that the small boat section serving the task force be under command of the task force commander or the United States Army Supply Forces rather than the navy. Conflicting and confusing orders and instructions were apparent during the campaign.

5. The determination of supply requirements and priority on shipment must rest with the task force commander rather than with the rear echelon.

6. In order to insure that adequate supply levels are maintained in the combat zone, a definite number of transport planes should be allotted permanently to the task force commander to fill his daily requirements and demands. Although it was agreed that fifteen (15) transport planes would be provided for daily maintenance (rations, ammunition and miscellaneous supplies) only on *one* occasion in two (2) months were deliveries made in the quantities specified and agreed upon.

7. It is vital that adequate service troops accompany the task force to the combat zone in order that supply dumps and bases may be established immediately. The use of combat troops for this purpose is wasteful to a point of negligence.

8. Transportation—motor, water, air, animal and human—

must be made available to the service troops of a task force to accomplish their assigned mission. The peculiarities of terrain, weather conditions and scope of operations will indicate the types and amount required.

9. Adequate guards and close supervision must be provided to eliminate pilfering of rations en route to front line troops. The following message from Headquarters, NGF, needs no amplification:

```
                                        New Guinea Force
                                        Headquarters,
ADV HQ NGF                              19 Jan, 43.
7 AUST DI
                    RATIONS FOR FORWARD AREA
```

1. Continual reports are reaching this HQ from various sources indicating that the rations received by the actual front-line soldier are still composed mainly of the more unpalatable portions of the ration, and that little jam, butter, or the more attractive tinned meats actually arrive in the front-line.

2. I have taken all possible steps to ensure that rations loaded from here are as varied and as attractive as possible, and the heads of the services concerned have given me an assurance that this is being carried out.

3. It is directed that you give what supervision is possible to ensure that units on the L of C do not pick the eyes out of the rations before they arrive at the front-line. It is suggested that disciplinary action might be taken in cases where definite evidence can be obtained of Offrs and ORs interfering with the ration supply.

```
                                    /s/ J. R. Broadbent
                                    ..............Brigadier
Distributed by "Q" to: 32 US Div    DA&QMG, NEW GUINEA FORCE
                      COSC Oro
```

10. Combat in a country where roads, bridges, trails and harbor facilities are nonexistent; where swamp lands are abundant; and where the countryside is subject to periodic floods by torrential rains, demands a maximum of engineering effort. A minimum of two engineer regiments (GS) in addition to organic troops should be made available to a division commander when conducting a campaign under such adverse conditions.

11. Conducting a campaign under conditions described in preceding paragraph requires a minimum of 2000 native laborers for supply, labor and evacuation purposes for a division. If native labor is nonexistent, additional service troops must be readily available for attachment to the division when the emergency arises, as it will beyond any doubt.

12. In combat operations where troops of two or more allied powers are engaged in accomplishing an assigned mission, it is highly desirable that a definite zone of operations—to include forward and rear supply installations—be assigned to the commander of troops of each allied power in accomplishing the common mission. This will eliminate misunderstanding and possible confusion.

The training, troop organization, staff procedure and teachings in the conduct of war are not identical in all nations. In combat, from the lowest ranks to the highest, there must be no doubt in the minds of troops as to the meaning of orders and directives of the commander. Long experience and training dictate that when troops are committed to action, all must "speak the same language".

The 2d Platoon, 2d Field Hospital before it was bombed.

. . .after it was bombed.

13. In areas where only rough trails and corduroy roads exist, battle casualties suffering from head, chest and abdominal wounds and fractures should be evacuated by litter bearers in order to reduce to a minimum the effect of shock.

14. The Geneva Cross displayed at hospitals is no guarantee of protection against deliberate enemy bombing. At 1125L on 7 December 1942 the Japanese bombed the 2d Platoon, 2d Field Hospital, which was located in an open kunai grass meadow south of Sinami Village. The bombing was repeated during the same day. Hospital tents and surrounding area were adequately and conspicuously marked with the Geneva Cross. The nearest combat troops were two (2) miles away which indicates beyond a reasonable doubt that the bombing was deliberate.

15. Troops in combat under conditions experienced in the Buna Campaign require additional medical troops with each battalion and higher unit. The portable hospital appears to be the answer.

16. A campaign conducted in an area separated by approximately 100 air and 450 nautical miles from its base must have a dependable and unfailing communications net. Duplicate radio equipment for communication between the task force commander and his base must be provided.

17. Dual wheel motor transportation is highly essential in areas subject to flood, mud and rain. Dual wheels on quarter-ton

jeeps greatly improved their performance during the Buna Campaign.

18. When naval craft operate in waters adjacent to coastlines held by a task force commander, the exchange of liaison officers is of paramount importance in order that information concerning movements and planned operations may be disseminated to both forces.

5 Inclosures:
 A- Ordnance Report
 B- Quartermaster Report
 C- Engineer Report
 D- Signal Report
 E- Medical Report

Appendix—Continued.

ANNEX #4
Inclosure A
Ordnance Report

1. AMMUNITION PLAN.

    a. The original ammunition plan was adequate. This plan called for 10 U/F, 5 units to be held in the SOS dumps, 3 units in corps, force or division dumps and 2 units in the hands of troops.

    b. Combat troops must use and think in terms of "Unit of Fire." It is not synonymous with the term "Day of Supply." It is not proper, after initial allocations have been made, to make allocations of ammunition for replenishment of stocks in terms of Units of Fire. Troops expend ammunition by round and require replenishment by rounds of specific type.

2. AMMUNITION SUPPLY.

    a. Ammunition can be resupplied successfully from what would be the equivalent of corps and army ASP's based solely upon the demands of divisions by rounds of specific type. The forms and many of the reports indicated in Field Maunuals 9-5, 11 July 1942 and 9-6, 29 July 1942, are not essentials in campaign. These forms and reports would later be of statistical and historical value. Their absence has made it difficult to draw definite conclusions regarding the rate of consumption of ammunition and documentation of historical records.

    b. Ammunition was resupplied primarily from the SOS dumps at Port Moresby based on daily radio requests from Headquarters Buna Forces (US). The Ordnance Officer of Buna Forces (US) received information daily by 'phone from battalions and separate companies as to their ammunition status. Attempt was made to supply ammunition in predetermined quantities and types but was abandoned 17 December 1942 after 10 days trial, because of frequent changes in requirements, air priorities, weather and other uncontrollable factors.

    c. The geographical location of the SOS ammunition dumps in the immediate vicinity of the rear detachment, 32d Division, simplified the administrative problem. Ammunition passed from SOS to combat troop control at the SOS dumps from which point it was trucked to either Ward's Drome or Seven Mile Drome and transported by air to Dobodura or Soputa.

    d. Dropping of ammunition without benefit of parachute from 'planes was found to be impracticable in that the ammunition might become distorted, a great deal lost or made hazardous for firing. All types of ammunition can be successfully dropped when parachute is used.

3. AMMUNITION EXPENDITURE.

    Ammunition consumed was limited to calibres .30, .45, 37mm, 60mm, 81mm, 105mm and fragmentation hand grenades. There follows a tabulation based on actual consumption by the Urbana Forces during the period 22 December 1942 to 10 January 1943.

ANNEX #4
Inclosure A

	* Unit of Fire	** One Day of Supply	Average One Days Exp. of Urbana Force	Ratio between Expenditure and	
				U/F	Day of Supply
60mm Mortar	5.6	7.5	5.9	1.05	.7
81mm Mortar	5.6	5.	18.5	3.3	3.7
Cal..30 Rifle	8.3	5.	11.8	1.4	2.6
Cal..30 MG	111.	150.	198.4	1.7	1.3
SMG	11.1	20.	18.	1.6	.9
Cal..50 MG	50.	90.	103.6	2.	1.1
37mm	5.5	20.	47.5	8.6	2.3
Grenade	8.3	4.5	22.5	2.5	5.
105mm How.	12.5	30.	65.	5.2	2.2

* Assumption made that 180 days supply of SA, mortar, AT and grenades equals 10 units of fire and 120 days supply of artillery equals 10 units of fire.
** Day of supply factor as set up by USASOS.

The consumption is higher than the World War I figures given in Paragraph 93, Field Manual 101-10 "Attack of Position." Offensive hand grenades could have been used had they been available. Unit of fire for offensive and fragmentation hand grenades should be .1 per individual per day in attack and not as so many per rifle company. At times any personnel available are employed in throwing hand grenades. The recommended breakdown of artillery fuzes is: for 75mm shell 60% time, 40% point detonating; for 105mm shell 40% time, 60% point detonating. The breakdown for 81mm mortar should be 50% heavy, 35% light, 15% smoke.

4. MAINTENANCE.

   a. The maintenance effort was found to be approximately 10% maintenance and 90% salvage. Maintenance personnel was attached direct to combat teams and until 3 January 1943 consisted of 1 officer, 10 ordnance armorers and 2 infantry mechanics on the Urbana Front, 1 officer, 8 ordnance armorers and 2 infantry mechanics on the Warren Front. These provided adequate maintenance but were inadequate for salvage operations and were reinforced by 1 officer and 20 ordnance armorers from Adv. Ech., Hq. 9th Ordnance Maintenance Battalion, Port Moresby.

   b. As of 8 January 1943 weapons being maintained in hands of troops on the Urbana Front were as follows:

   1547 rifles M1   6 cal. .50 machine guns
    173 rifles 03   22 - 60mm mortars
     42 BAR's   22 - 81mm mortars
     43 light machine guns 208 sub-machine guns
      6 heavy machine guns   2 - 37mm AT guns

As stated above this force was being serviced by 1 officer and 12 enlisted men who were reinforced by 6 armorers as of 3 January 1943. These weapons were all that remained in combat from the original equipment of the 2d Battalion, 126th Infantry, 1st, 2d and 3d Battalions, 127th Infantry, Cannon Co. and 2d Battalion, 128th Infantry. The difference between the quantities shown and the original equipment represented to a great extent the scope of the salvage operations on that front. It is estimated the average combatant personnel on this front was 2200 during the period 22 December 1942 to 3 January 1943, both dates inclusive.

Ordnance Salvage Dump in rear of Urbana Command Post.

    c. Repair facilities consisted only of hand tools.

    d. Unusual demands were made for main recoil springs for sub-machine gun, rear sight and bolt assemblies calibre .30 M1 rifle, driving springs and cocking levers for light machine gun M1919A4, firing pins for both 60mm and 81mm mortar, oiler and thong cases, brushes and cleaning rods, cleaning and preserving materials. Ordnance supplies, both major items and expendable materials, passed from SOS control to Ground Forces at the SOS dumps in the same manner as ammunition.

5. SUPPLY AND EVACUATION.

    a. In lieu of service troops which were not provided, it was discovered there were enough casuals in the rear areas to meet any unusual demands for labor. These casuals flow from hospitals en route to front. They were marked "duty" but were not entirely fit for combat.

    b. Transport of supplies by air is probably the most inefficient and uneconomical operation. The lift of the largest cargo planes available equals only the payload of the 2½ ton truck.

    c. The practice of evacuating enemy materiel, ammunition and documents thru Australian channels seriously hampered the Ground Forces and the Services of Supply in obtaining valuable technical information. The above practice delayed report on enemy alleged explosive bullet to the Chief Ordnance Officer until 26 December 1942. This matter has been made subject of separate correspondence between Chief Ordnance Officer, USASOS, SWPA, and the Chief of Ordnance under date of 16 January 1943, and separate report by Corps Ordnance Officer to Commanding General, I Corps dated 8 January 1943 Subject: "Alleged Explosive Bullet - Enemy Ammunition." It appears from these findings that the Japanese have found a means of avoiding International Treaties while complying with the letter of agreements regarding use of the dum-dum bullet. This should be of interest to all Allied Nations.

6. VEHICLES.

The only vehicles in use at the front were the jeep and the 1-ton trailer. During the relatively dry season the jeeps were operated with standard tires. As the rainy season advanced, two methods of giving greater flotation were used. In one method the command car tires were mounted on jeep wheels. In the second method dual wheels were constructed for the rear axle of the jeep. Standard jeep tires were used. This second method appeared more satisfactory than the first and was an important factor in the supply system from Dobodura forward.

7. GENERAL OBSERVATIONS.

a. The Browning automatic rifle was found to be too heavy, clumsy and difficult to maintain. It was in most cases discarded by the using personnel in favor of some other weapons.

b. The sub-machine gun and the light machine gun M1919A4 were the most popular weapons.

c. Need for a telescopically equipped calibre .30 target rifle for sniping was indicated.

d. Jungle knives and bayonets were not used in combat.

e. Tracer ammunition for ground targets was not used since it disclosed positions to enemy. The tracer rounds were withdrawn by combat troops from machine gun belts and ball rounds substituted.

f. The 37mm canister was decidedly effective against personnel in the open and became a very popular round when targets presented themselves. From experimental firing it appears the canister has a spread of 1 ft. for every 6 ft. of range covering an area of 100 ft. at 200 yds.

g. The 81mm high explosive round, heavy, was quite effective and demoralizing to the enemy. Limited firings were conducted at Port Moresby with the same lot number reported as giving excessive number of duds. No duds occurred during these firings. It is believed that the report was made where the rounds were falling in very soft ground or swamp so that the sound of the explosions could not be heard and very little crater effect caused. The 81mm heavy round when fitted with non delay fuze is a highly efficient "daisy-cutter".

h. The Australian anti-personnel rifle grenade is considered as very good.

i. Offensive hand grenades if available could have been used with effect at times.

Appendix--Continued.

ANNEX #4
Inclosure B
Quartermaster Report

The lessons learned by the Quartermaster, I Corps, during the period Dec 1, 1942 - Jan 24, 1943, in the campaign to reduce the Buna-Gona-Sanananda area, fall within the following three basic categories:

1. Leadership.
2. Supply and Transportation.
3. Morale.

LEADERSHIP - Much has been said about the absolute need for trained leadership in battle and the failure of leadership in some units during the campaign. More may be said. It is desired to point out here that trained leadership is as essential to prompt and adequate supply as it is to tactical success, and, axiomatically, success in supply is necessary before tactical success can be expected. There were no individuals of the several QM units involved who failed in their individual missions or assignments, but there were some, notably among commissioned officers, who did poorer work than others. Without exception these individuals were those who had been transferred to supply work after having been trained for one line branch or other. It is of paramount importance for future operations that all such individuals be weeded out and returned to their initial branches or reclassified.

SUPPLY AND TRANSPORTATION - Logistically the campaign was a nightmare. Ineptitude played as big a part in the supply difficulties as did the physical conditions encountered.

On December 1 it was found that US troops were subsisting on 1/3 of a "C" ration and 1/6 of a "D" ration per day. The "D" ration was not always available. This had been going on for approximately one week. Caloric content of this ration approximates 1000 calories, and the stockage of food for the 32d Division north of the Owen Stanley Range was reported as 1½ days. The Comdg General, I Corps, immediately directed that a full "C" ration be used. At this time supply for the division, except for the Warren Force, was by air from Port Moresby. The essential problem involved was getting more food over the mountains. Within a short time a conference was arranged with the Chief of Staff, Adv NGF, and the minimum essential daily requirements for US troops was set up. Assurance was given that this minimum daily maintenance would be transported daily, or made up on following days if air transportation became unavailable on any day. The system worked for about a week. Thereafter constantly repeated requests to NGF had to be made in order to keep food stockages up to reasonable levels. Fortunately, there had been transported in one day approximately 200,000 lbs of food (40,000 rations), and this reserve was never completely exhausted for the rest of the campaign. A trip back to Port Moresby, where a conference was had with the Quartermaster there and the S-4, resulted in the formulation of a well balanced diet, which it was agreed would be supplied thereafter. The diet consisted of a "B" ration supplemented by added fruits, fruit juices, and bulky items. Due to controls exerted by NGF the ration was changed shortly after its establishment.

On December 1 the depot at Dobodura was manned entirely by Engineer personnel from the 32d Division. The Division Engineer supervised all supply activities, and part of one company, commanded by a Captain of the Engineers, did the actual work.* It is no criticism of the Division Engineer establishment or the individuals to say that they were inadequate for the job. They had not been trained in supply work. After the Dobodura depot was organized it was found that approximately 20,000 "D" rations and 5,000 "C" rations were on hand, of which they had no knowledge. These rations were found scattered throughout the area in small quantities. Some of them had been ruined by improper storage. This instance is pointed out to emphasize that Quartermaster supply is specialized and that no one or no establishment can accomplish it properly except trained Quartermaster personnel. To correct the condition four officers and forty-four EM of the 116th Quartermaster Battalion were flown over from Port Moresby. Additional personnel was required and these were obtained from casuals and detachments of the several service companies of the division. Additional jeep transportation was called for and was received. Supply was put on a practicable basis.

G-4 Section arranged with the Corps Ordnance Officer to equip jeeps in the Buna area with rear dual tires and with oversize tires. The result of this experiment was very satisfactory. It will be reported on elsewhere.

Landing supplies at Hariko.

Supply of the 32d Division was shifted from Dobodura to Hariko on or about January 5. Supplies were to be shipped from Oro Bay by water, and there unloaded and distributed to the division. Actually Hariko served not only as a supply base for the 32d Division, but also for the 7th Australian Division. With approximately 80 EM and 5 officers, the Quartermaster establishment unloaded the supplies under almost unbelievable conditions, and successfully stored and distributed them.

See Incl "C", Annex 4.

Varying numbers of natives were used in supply and evacuation during the period, the number at no time exceeding 1,000, and toward the end of the campaign was standardized at 700. Were it not for the availability of natives supply would have fallen down badly. At times, distribution in its entirety was dependent upon them. This point is brought out to emphasize the need for a complete Quartermaster establishment in any operational area. If natives, properly organized, can be obtained in future operations they can be used to supplement organic establishments. Planning should, however, envisage the utilization of the organic Quartermaster companies of divisions in their entirety. There was never enough Quartermaster personnel north of the Owen Stanley Range. It may be argued that the job was done and done well. The fact remains, however, that a better job could have been done had there been more service personnel available.

Quartermaster personnel performed duties of the Transportation Corps, the Ordnance Department, the Postal Service, and to a limited degree the Medical Department during the operations just completed. It is obvious that insofar as time and energy of Quartermaster personnel was required in these duties, that personnel was handicapped in the performance of its own functional duties. It is recommended that hereafter sufficient personnel of other services and supply branches be so placed in the combat zone that they may do the work for which they are intended, thus relieving Quartermaster personnel to add to the quality and extent of their service of the troops.

During actual combat the requests for clothing and equipment were few. By the time combat was over it had become practicable to move into the Dobodura depot most of the essential requirements. There was, however, no stock of any kind on December 1.

Much of the difficulty of supply was occasioned by the mixed administration, Australian and American. While this is not intended as a criticism of Australian personnel or command, it is emphasized that our allies are not familiar with our requirements or methods of supply, and secondly, do not have the same degree of interest in supplying our troops as we have ourselves. This is but natural and human. In future operations it is deemed highly desirable that US troops have a complete supply and administrative set-up of their own, rather than be dependent upon someone else.

MORALE - The problem of morale is vitally linked with that of leadership and supply. It is desired to emphasize the following points, however:

Mail Service - There were many tons of mail accumulated at Port Moresby on December 8. Why it had not been sent to the organization is beside the point. The fact is that arrangements were made immediately for the transmission of this mail to the combat area, where Quartermaster personnel proceeded to handle and distribute it for the next six weeks. The effect on the morale of the troops was immediately apparent.*

Gratuitous Issue - A constant struggle was necessary to get "gratuitous issue items" to the soldiers. Large quantities of these items were on hand at Port Moresby. It is a fact that no razor blades had been distributed for approximately six weeks prior to

*See Annex 1.

December 10. No tooth brushes or tooth paste or shaving cream had been received or distributed. Cigarette issues were pitifully small and far apart. When the gratuitous issue items were finally received the effect on the morale was remarkable. It is believed that the use of the term "gratuitous issue items" should be discontinued wherever US troops are dependent upon Australian command or supply agencies. The items should be included in the ration and so considered.

Food - It would seem to be unnecessary to speak of food under the general heading of morale, but the fact remains that on December 1, officers and men of the 32d Division, exclusive of the Warren Force, showed the results of malnutrition. There can be little doubt that the temporary failure of the 32d Division to accomplish tactical missions was due largely to the emaciated condition of the troops. Within 48 hours of the time that they were supplied a proper ration they showed more fighting spirit. That the psychological effect of an adequate diet was as improtant as the physical effect connot be denied. Planning for future operations should be so precise that failure of food supply will be impossible.

Appendix--Continued.

ANNEX #4
Inclosure C
Engineer Report

The operations of the engineer battalion throughout the Papuan Campaign are summarized as follows:

  a. Selection of sites, preparation and operation of air strips at Dobodura and Pongani.

  b. Organization and operation of supply base at Dobodura from 21 November to 12 December for both Australian and U. S. Troops.

  c. Feeding and housing of all casuals, both American and Australian passing through Dobodura.

  d. Evacuation of wounded initially at Hariko and later at Dobodura.

  e. Burial of the dead. One cemetery established at Hariko and one at Dobodura.

  f. Control and administration of native labor assigned to the division.

  g. Establishment and operation of a salvage dump and ordnance repair depot at Dobodura from 21 November to 12 December.

  h. Disposal of unexploded bombs, mines and duds throughout the campaign.

  i. Assisting in unloading and moving of Australian light tanks.

  j. Construction and maintenance of over 30 miles of roads and trails, including the following:

    (1) Construction of 4 miles of jeep corduroy.
    (2) Construction of 3.75 miles of class 12 (12 ton) corduroy.
    (3) Construction of 11 foot bridges total length 1675 feet.
    (4) Construction of 23 class 12 culverts.
    (5) Construction of 2 class 5 (5 ton) bridges total length 350 feet.
    (6) Construction of 4 class 12 bridges, total length 280 feet.
    (7) Clearing 300,000 square yards of grass and jungle.
    (8) Construction of 30 ton pile and trestle bend bridge at Horanda, total length 395 feet.

NATIVE LABOR:

  The success of engineer operations in this campaign was due, in no small way, to the loyal, wholehearted and tireless efforts

Building jeep-track from Sinemi Village to bridge between the strips...

... a completed section.

of the natives assigned to this work. The number of natives assigned varied in accordance with the situation and at one time over 1000 natives were on engineer work. Best results were obtained by segregating the natives so that those assigned to any one project were all of the same tribe. After a little experience, one soldier can efficiently control about 20 natives and in some cases one NCO handled as many as 50. It was found that by marking out the days work and instructing the natives as to the limit of their task, more work could be accomplished than otherwise. In assigning natives to tasks, it is well to remember that tribes whose villages are located in low swampy areas, must know something about stream crossings and are therefore the bridge builders; while those whose villages are on high ground must know something about traversing hills and are therefore the road builders. The natives were often consulted in the matter of selecting trees, bark, and vines to be used in construction projects.

JAPANESE BUNKERS:

Exterior of typical Japanese bunker. Note soldier on left.

In the Buna Area, the terrain--with rare exception more than two or three feet above sea level--precluded the use of the deep trench or dugout of World War I. As a solution to this difficulty the Japanese built bunkers. These bunkers consisted of two general types:

(1) The large, heavily bolstered bunkers located in more or less open terrain (i.e. coconut groves, edges of air strips, etc.); and

(2) Smaller, less heavily bolstered bunkers and fox holes located in terrain the thickness of which precluded the use of accompanying weapons and precision bombing.

These two types of bunkers had in common shallow trenches for foundations, excellent camouflage, thick over-head cover of palm logs and connecting nets of fire trenches.

Not all bunkers had fire slits and none had enough to accommodate the number of personnel the bunker was capable of holding. Primarily, the enemy used bunkers for shelters during artillery and mortar barrages, or air raids; and, secondarily, as firing positions.

Interior of Japanese bunker.

Interior of bunker reinforced with sand filled oil drums.

If bunker locations did not have a natural field of fire, one was seldom cleared. Snipers in nearby trees acted as observers and directed what fire was being delivered from the bunkers.

CONSTRUCTION OF BUNKERS:

Both the large and the small bunkers were built along the same general lines with the large bunkers, of course, being more elaborate. Using a shallow trench for a foundation, log columns and beams were erected, log reveting walls built and a ceiling course strung using several layers of logs running laterally to the trench. With the completion of this basic superstructure, the reveting walls were reinforced variously by sheets of iron, steel drums filled with sand, ammunition boxes filled with sand and additional piles of logs. Lastly, the entire superstructure was covered with a bursting course of earth, rocks, coconuts and short pieces of log. For camouflage, the surface of the finished bunker was planted with fast-growing vegetation.

The finished interior of the larger bunkers varied from four to six feet in height, six to ten feet in width, and twelve to thirty feet in length.

Different bunkers used different types of entrances. Some used direct openings from fire trenches, others used tunnels. In all but the rarest exceptions, these openings were trapped or angled in such a way that the explosion of a grenade inside the opening would not injure personnel in the bunker.

Some few bunkers were used to shelter accompanying weapons such as antitank guns. These bunkers usually had large direct openings.

Japanese Mountain Gun in bunker near Giropa Point.

Fox holes in general were merely shallow holes in the ground with built-up sides and a covering of logs and earth, or coral rock and earth. All were well camouflaged and a majority had fire slits of some kind.

CONCLUSIONS AND RECOMMENDATIONS:

Throughout the campaign there was constant demand for more and more engineers and the tasks assigned the engineer battalion would have kept a full regiment constantly busy. It is recommended that for this type of warfare engineer units be made an organic part of each infantry regiment, and that the engineer combat battalion be left intact under division control. The tremendous problem of establishing and maintaining supply routes would alone justify this change.

The division engineer was not consulted until the campaign was well under way, and it was on 28 October, that he received orders to proceed from Australia to Port Moresby along with the assistant division engineer. Shortly after his arrival in Papua the division engineer was confronted with the problem of operating a 2 company battalion without the assistance of his staff, and this condition existed until 26 December.

When infantry units have no tasks for attached engineers, they should be released for duty elsewhere. The 1st Platoon of Company "A" used as a carrying party by the 2d Bn, CT 126 from 21 November to 24 December would have been better occupied had it rejoined the company on the Ango-Buna Mission road tasks. The use of engineers for handling supplies, burying the dead and evacuating the wounded at Dobodura and Hariko surely reduced the number available for work on the 23 miles of jeep trails for which the battalion was responsible.

Engineer troops must do more marching during training periods and this should be done with full jungle equipment, including one engineer tool such as a shovel, axe, saw, etc. Some consideration should be given, relative to reducing the weight of tools to be used in jungle warfare. Troops should be armed with the carbine in lieu of the M-1 rifle. Gas-operated saws would speed up the job of procuring timber for corduroy and bridges. Obviously, if native labor is to be used, many additional tools must be procured. Engineers should receive early priority in the issue of jeeps during jungle operations as they are essential to the movement of tools and supplies. Although water purification sets were available in rear areas, they were not brought forward because all available space on transport planes was used for supplies of a more vital nature. Water could be readily found within 1 or 2 feet of the ground surface and individual procurement and purification worked out very well. The class 12 corduroy roads (12-ton capacity), were placed at the rate of 1/3 yard per man per day using troops and natives in the ratio of about 1 to 4. This includes the procurement of timber with an average hand carry haul of 500 yards.

Appendix—Continued.

ANNEX #4
Inclosure D
Signal Report

The following comments outline the salient features of Signal Communication experience gained in the Buna Campaign.

1. MESSAGE CENTER:

   a. The Signal Company did not have sufficient personnel provided by Tables of Organization to operate continuously in a satisfactory manner.

   b. Large amounts of cryptographed traffic were handled due to the required increased use of radio. Numerically reciphered division field codes and numerically reciphered Australian codes were used extensively. These systems have proven their worth and can be operated rapidly with proper training, especially the Australian type.

   c. The Division Field Code in its present form is not made of material durable for jungle operations. Also the vocabulary should be increased.

   d. The need of some mechanical cryptographic system cannot be overemphasized. The use of the cipher device M-209 or the cipher device M-134 would have materially reduced the number of personnel required for cryptographic work. These devices are authorized for division but were not available to troops in the Buna Campaign. In spite of the success of the reciphered codes used, much additional and vital speed could have been gained had the mechanical equipment been available.

2. MESSENGER COMMUNICATION:

   a. The organization of messenger service as ordinarily employed could not cope with the situation. In many instances motor vehicles could not be used. Distances and terrain difficulties were too great to rely on dismounted messengers as a substitute means. There is a definite need for a light vehicle of some type to negotiate native tracks. Perhaps a bicycle with a small motor mounted in the frame could be made to fill this requirement.

3. RADIO COMMUNICATION:

   a. Radio was the main communication link back to rear areas and supply bases.

   b. The Radio Set SCR-188 handled the bulk of the traffic from Buna Force Headquarters to Port Moresby.

   c. The performance of the Radio Set SCR-193 was very satisfactory.

   d. The Radio Set SCR-284 proved to be too bulky and heavy to be transported by the operating personnel on foot.

e. Two standard 1/4 ton, 4 x 4 trucks, modified to accomodate Radio Set SCR-193, were flown to the Buna area to provide alternate radio channels to the rear echelon at Port Moresby. All three circuits were frequently required to clear traffic for GHQ, New Guinea Force, I Corps, Seventh Australian Division, and the 32d U. S. Division. These sets were separated by a minimum of 100 yards and were available on a moment's notice in case of failure of regularly used radio sets.

f. All low powered radios were appreciably affected by the attenuation due to absorption by dense tropical vegetation.

g. Radio operators during the first stages of the campaign clearly evidenced the fact that insufficient training had been given on actual field radio nets under simulated battle conditions and that the majority of training had been devoted to the code table.

4. WIRE COMMUNICATION:

a. Telephone

(1) The use of wire assumed its place of prime importance throughout the entire campaign and was as extensive as the tropical terrain allowed. Every possible use of simplex and phantom circuits was made to supplement the much needed physical circuits.

Buna Force (US) switchboard near Sinemi Village.

(2) Two lines were laid from the Buna Force Headquarters, Sinemi, to each of the front-line infantry regiments. A switching central was installed at Dobodura from which lines were run to each of four air strips, to aircraft warning posts and to Advanced Headquarters, New Guinea Force. All field and portable hospitals and supply bases at Hariko and Oro Bay were also given wire lines. An artillery switching central was later set up with

lines to each of the Australian and American artillery batteries.

(3) A total of approximately 300 miles of field wire was used during the operation, all of which was laid by hand. A large percentage of this wire was installed by the signal company from RL-27-A axles or improvised bamboo axles carried by hand. In impassable terrain, parties often laid wire along stream banks while floating down stream on rafts.

(4) As a result of the limited wire service, lines were made to serve in dual capacity. For example: When the artillery fired, it became necessary to allocate talking circuits for the exclusive use of fire control.

(5) Combat wire W-130 proved its worth in forward areas during the attack stages. Its early replacement by wire W-110-B is important if service is to be depended upon.

(6) Wire maintenance was made difficult by sniping, bombing, strafing and wire cutting by isolated enemy parties. In some cases friendly native carriers cut out sections of wire to secure their supplies. At night, wire parties sometimes were fired on by friendly troops. Wire parties also showed inexperience in night operations by their inability to find their way in the dense darkness of the jungle.

(7) The maintenance of wire lines was enhanced by the introduction of numerous test points.

(8) Considerable difficulty was experienced in the forward areas with shorts in the telephone EE-8-A due to corrosion of the contacts of the handset switch.

(9) The material used in the construction of the jack assembly of switchboard unit EE-2-C appears to be inferior and numerous instances of trouble were experienced because of rusting and early fatigue in spring contacts. While the housing provided for the drop windings and armature of EE-2-C is a very desirable improvement over the unprotected drop assembly in the EE-2-B, the latter unit is considered generally far superior.

(10) Moisture condensation within the case of the coil C-114 caused numerous line shorts.

b. **Teletype**

(1) A teletype net was established with an instrument at Headquarters Buna Force, Sinemi; Advance New Guinea Force, Dobodura; Hariko and Oro Bay.

5. **SIGNAL SUPPLY AND MAINTENANCE:**

a. Equipment had to be serviced every day. Lack of training in this respect lost or rendered useless much signal equipment which was costly in time and cargo space to replace. The extreme dampness of tropical climate requires that equipment be thoroughly sunned and dried daily. When this policy was adopted, equipment failures were appreciably reduced. In numerous instances men carelessly allowed their equipment to become wet, damaged, or lost.

b. During most of the operations, signal supplies had

to be transported by air. This fact, coupled with unusually difficult factors of maintenance and repair, created a hand-to-mouth supply situation which at times became acute.

    c. Such vital supplies as batteries were delivered loose and were frequently rendered useless by moisture absorption. These and other similar type supplies should be delivered to forward areas in suitable water-tight cartons so as to afford protection from moisture until required.

    d. At times the supply of wire was diminished to the point where it became necessary to salvage combat wire to maintain communication.

6. <u>GENERAL</u>:

    a. The need for a form of lightweight shelter to provide housing for radio stations and telephone switchboards in the tropics must not be overlooked. Heavy rainfall and normal high humidities rendered useless appreciable quantities of signal equipment.

Typical field switchboard installation.

    b. In the tropics, kerosene or gasoline lanterns radiate too much heat to permit proper working conditions in blacked-out message center, telegraph, radio, and telephone tents. Electric lighting provided the solution to this problem, but additional lamps, sockets and wire are needed.

    c. Radio and wire each retained their important roles in jungle warfare. Low powered radio sets within the division could not replace wire due to the atmospheric and terrain difficulties encountered. On the other hand the distances to established bases were such that medium and high powered radio sets furnished the most feasible means of communication since the required wire lines over these distances would often have been impracticable if not impossible.

Appendix—Continued.

ANNEX #4
Inclosure E
Medical Report

1. <u>AIR EVACUATION</u>.

During the Buna Campaign, all casualties were evacuated from the front to Port Moresby by air transportation. It was noted that when air transports arrived at Wards Drome, no one knew whether patients were aboard. It was taken for granted that patients were aboard; consequantly, ambulances would follow the transport to the various dispersal bays. Many transports returned without patients. Through cooperation with the air service, a simple system was devised. The pilot displayed a white or red flag which indicated that he had patients aboard; the white flag indicating walking patients, the red flag indicating litter cases. By this simple expedient, it could be easily determined the number of ambulances to follow the plane to its dispersal bay.

2. <u>EVACUATION POLICY</u>.

To conserve the fighting strength of the 32 Division the policy which required the evacuation to Australia of all patients whose hospitalization would require over 7 days was amended to 30 days. The 30-day policy was announced in a General Order late in December, 1942.

3. <u>INADEQUATE HOSPITAL FACILITIES</u>.

During the first week in December, the 10th Evacuation Hospital arrived in Port Moresby and absorbed the hospital facilities of the Provisional Medical Battalion. By the 15th of December, the 171st Station Hospital, a 500-bed unit, had arrived at Port Moresby and was established a short distance from Koki Mission. Thus it will be seen that in a period of 3 weeks, the bed capacity of the hospitals in New Guinea expanded from approximately 700 to 2428. About January 15, 1943, the 135th Medical Regiment at Port Moresby arrived and began to erect a type of convalescent camp.

4. <u>MEDICAL SUPPLY</u>.

a. Medical supplies as a whole, were excellent and adequate. To simplify distribution of medical supplies to the various battalion and regimental aid stations and portable surgical hospitals attached to the 32d Division, all medical supplies were sent to the 2d Platoon, 2d Field Hospital, at Dobodura.

b. Some difficulty was experienced in returning litters to the combat area. This was principally due to the fact that on many occasions, the pilots did not know until just before the take-off, whether they were to land at Dobodura or Popondetta. This difficulty was overcome later by delivering the litters to the Assistant G-4 of the 32d Division, who had definite knowledge of the destination of the planes.

5. **COMMUNICABLE DISEASES.**

During December the first cases of malaria in the 32 Division began to make their appearance. Many patients were admitted to hospital with the diagnosis of "fever, undetermined origin". The majority of the cases later proved to be malaria. During the period December 8, 1942, to and including January 26, 1943, there were 637 cases of malaria and 3216 cases of fever, undetermined origin. There were approximately 18 cases of typhus fever with 7 deaths. In the Corps Surgeon's Annual Report to the Surgeon General, it was recommended that troops destined for Australia and the Far East be not given typhus innoculations as the typhus vaccine given in the United States is specifically for the European typhus.

6. **CASUALTIES - 32d DIVISION - BUNA CAMPAIGN**, 26 September 1942 - 28 February 1943.

Type of Casualty	126 Inf CT	127 Inf CT	128 Inf CT	Fwd & Rear Ech	TOTALS
Killed in Action	266	182	138	16	602
Died of Wounds	34	29	25	0	88
Died of Other Causes	5	3	4	5	17
Total Deaths	305	214	167	21	707
Wounded in Action, Gunshot Wounds	475	308	279	6	1068
Wounded in Action, Shrapnel Wounds	253	196	155	8	612
Total Wounds	728	504	434	14	1680
Fevers, Including Malaria	1422	2011	1264	661	5358
Common Diarrheas	170	123	205	65	563
Shell Shock & Concussion	35	89	87	0	211
Misc Diseases	658	590	682	224	2154
Total Diseases	2285	2813	2238	950	8286
Total Injuries	88	57	123	19	287
GRAND TOTALS	3406	3588	2962	1004	10960

The above data was obtained from medical and personnel records of the 32d Division. There were, in addition to the above, sixty-two (62) missing in action, according to personnel records.

7. **INADEQUATE RATIONS.**

The ration for troops and patients, sometimes unpalatable, was routinely without variety; patients frequently were fed with foods which were difficult for a healthy soldier to consume; canned milk was available in wholly inadequate quantities; fresh meats, vegetables and fruit were rarely available even in the hospitals. It is believed that until such time as fresh meats, fruits and vegetables are available for all troops in New Guinea, multivitamin capsules should be provided daily. Refrigeration was woefully lacking at the hospitals where it presented a serious deficiency, for fevers are prevalent and ice is a tremendous asset to an adequate medical program.

8. LESSONS LEARNED.

    a. Earlier planning for the hospitalization of sick and wounded should be provided prior to active combat. The movement of combat troops and hospital facilities should be simultaneous.

    b. In addition to one portable surgical hospital per battalion combat team, it is recommended that 3 additional portable surgical hospitals should be assigned to each division. The additional 3 portable surgical hospitals would be used as a reserve and to provide replacements for both commissioned and enlisted personnel. They could also be used to hospitalize patients in the event evacuation is delayed.

    c. To provide for each regimental combat team of the 32d Division, the clearing company of the 107th Medical Battalion was divided into 3 platoons. As the clearing company of a medical battalion, according to present T/O and T/BA, provides only for 2 platoons, it is urgently recommended that an additional platoon, complete in personnel and equipment, be added to the present clearing company. This would enable each regimental combat team to have a complete clearing platoon.

    d. As the Buna Campaign was fought in the world's most heavily infested malaria region, greater stress should be applied for the preventive treatment of malaria. In addition to the suppressive drugs, it is believed that more liberal and frequent application of repellents should be used.

    e. In the future the supply of better foods in greater quantity and variety must receive more positive attention. Refrigeration, which is a definite essential to proper hospitalization, must be provided in greater quantities.

REPRODUCED BY 69TH ENGINEER CO.,(TOP.) U.S. ARMY

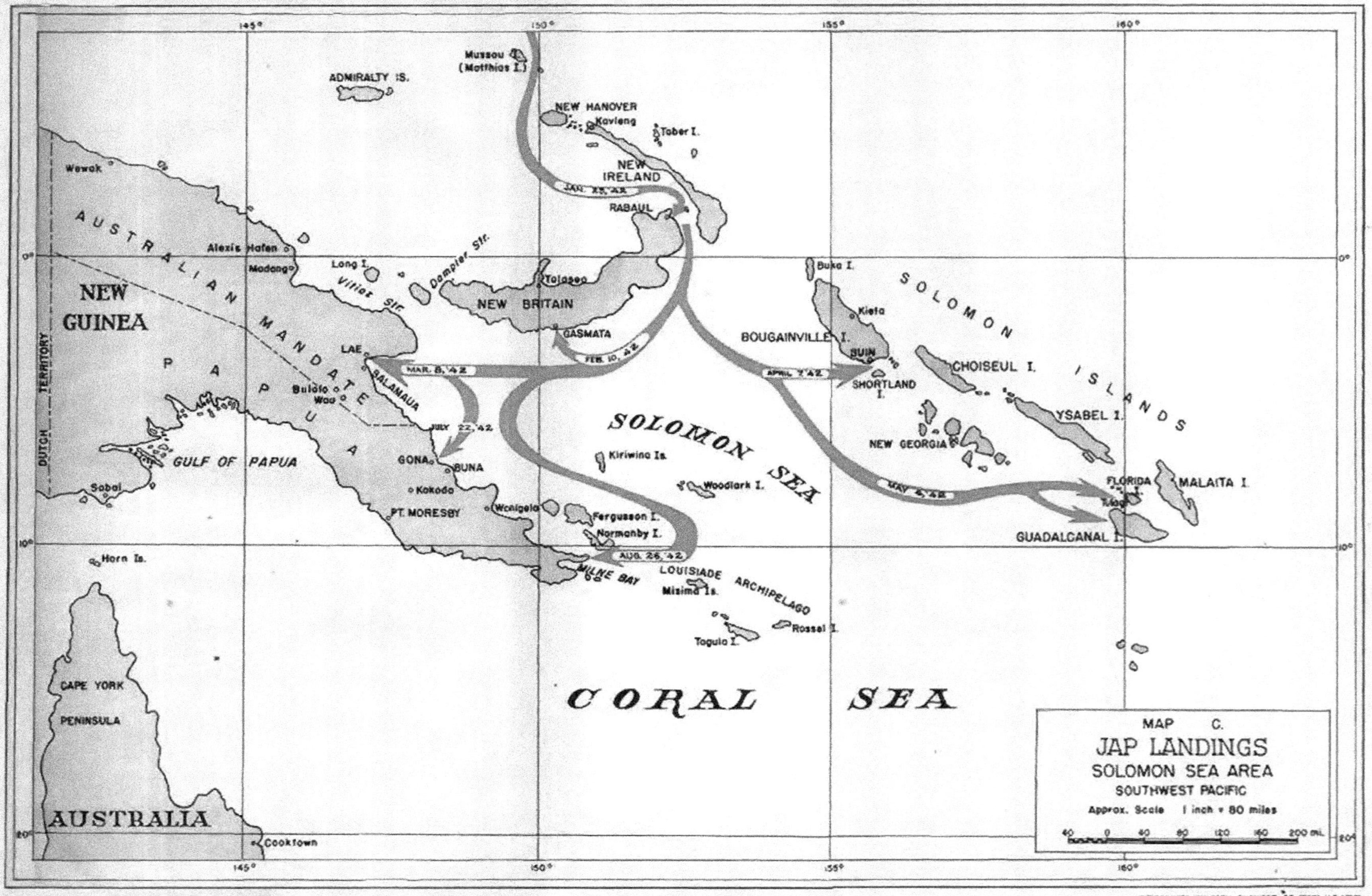
MAP C.
JAP LANDINGS
SOLOMON SEA AREA
SOUTHWEST PACIFIC
Approx. Scale 1 inch = 80 miles
40 0 40 80 120 160 200 mi.
ADMIRALTY IS.
Mussau (Matthias I.)
NEW HANOVER
Kavieng
Tabar I.
NEW IRELAND
RABAUL
JAN. 23, 42
NEW BRITAIN
Talasea
GASMATA
FEB. 10, 42
Dampier Str.
Vitiaz Str.
Long I.
Wewak
Alexis Hafen
Madang
NEW GUINEA
AUSTRALIAN MANDATE
PAPUA
DUTCH TERRITORY
LAE
SALAMAUA
MAR. 8, 42
Bulolo
Wau
JULY 22, 42
GONA
BUNA
Kokoda
PT. MORESBY
Wanigela
GULF OF PAPUA
Sabai
Horn Is.
CAPE YORK PENINSULA
AUSTRALIA
Cooktown
SOLOMON SEA
Kiriwina Is.
Woodlark I.
Fergusson I.
Normanby I.
AUG. 26, 42
MILNE BAY
LOUISIADE ARCHIPELAGO
Misima Is.
Tagula I.
Rossel I.
CORAL SEA
SOLOMON ISLANDS
Buka I.
Kieta
BOUGAINVILLE I.
BUIN
APRIL 7, 42
SHORTLAND I.
CHOISEUL I.
YSABEL I.
NEW GEORGIA
MAY 4, 42
FLORIDA
Tulagi
MALAITA I.
GUADALCANAL I.
145°
150°
155°
160°
0°
10°
20°
REPRODUCED BY 59TH ENGINEER CO.(TOP) U.S.ARMY

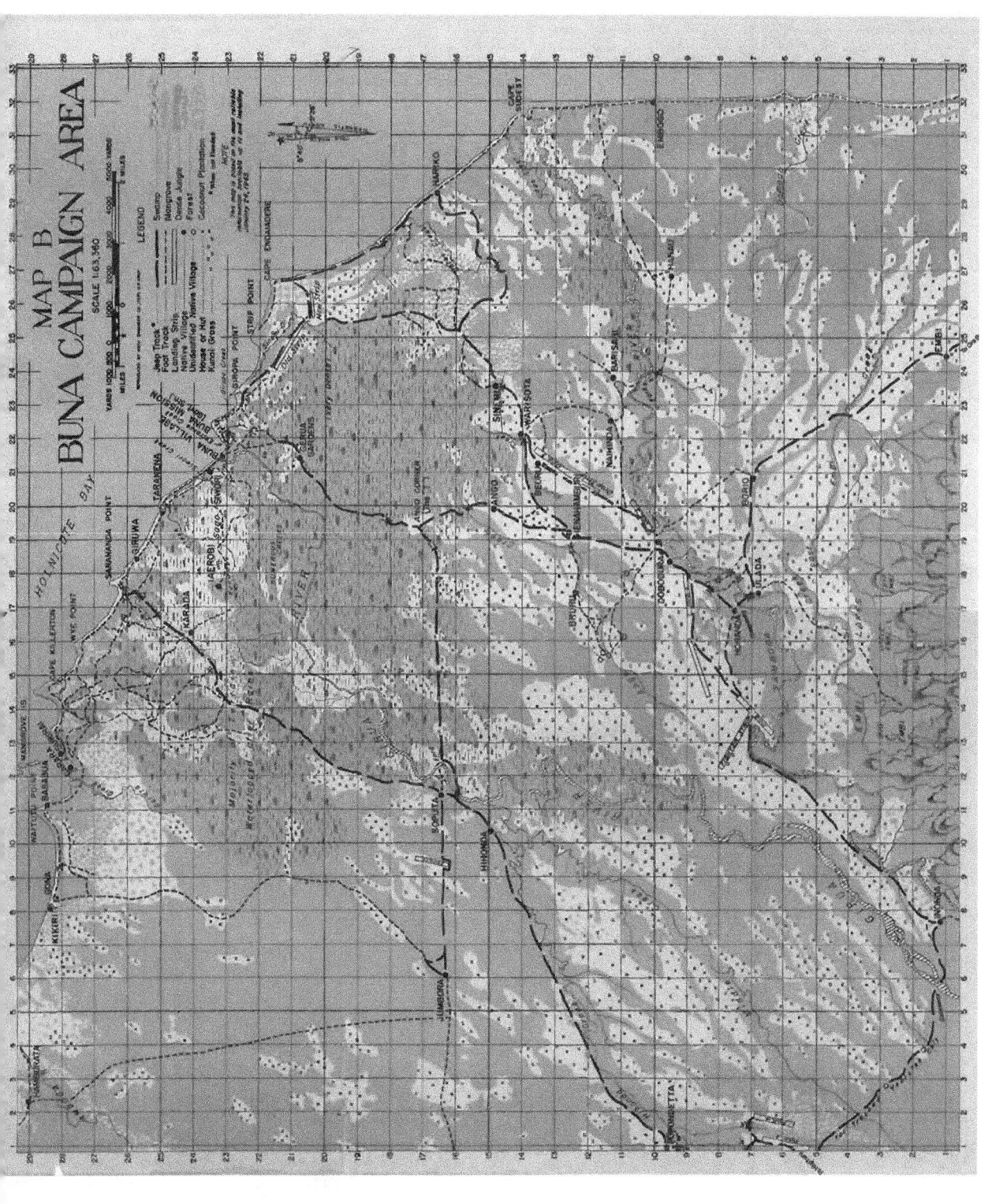

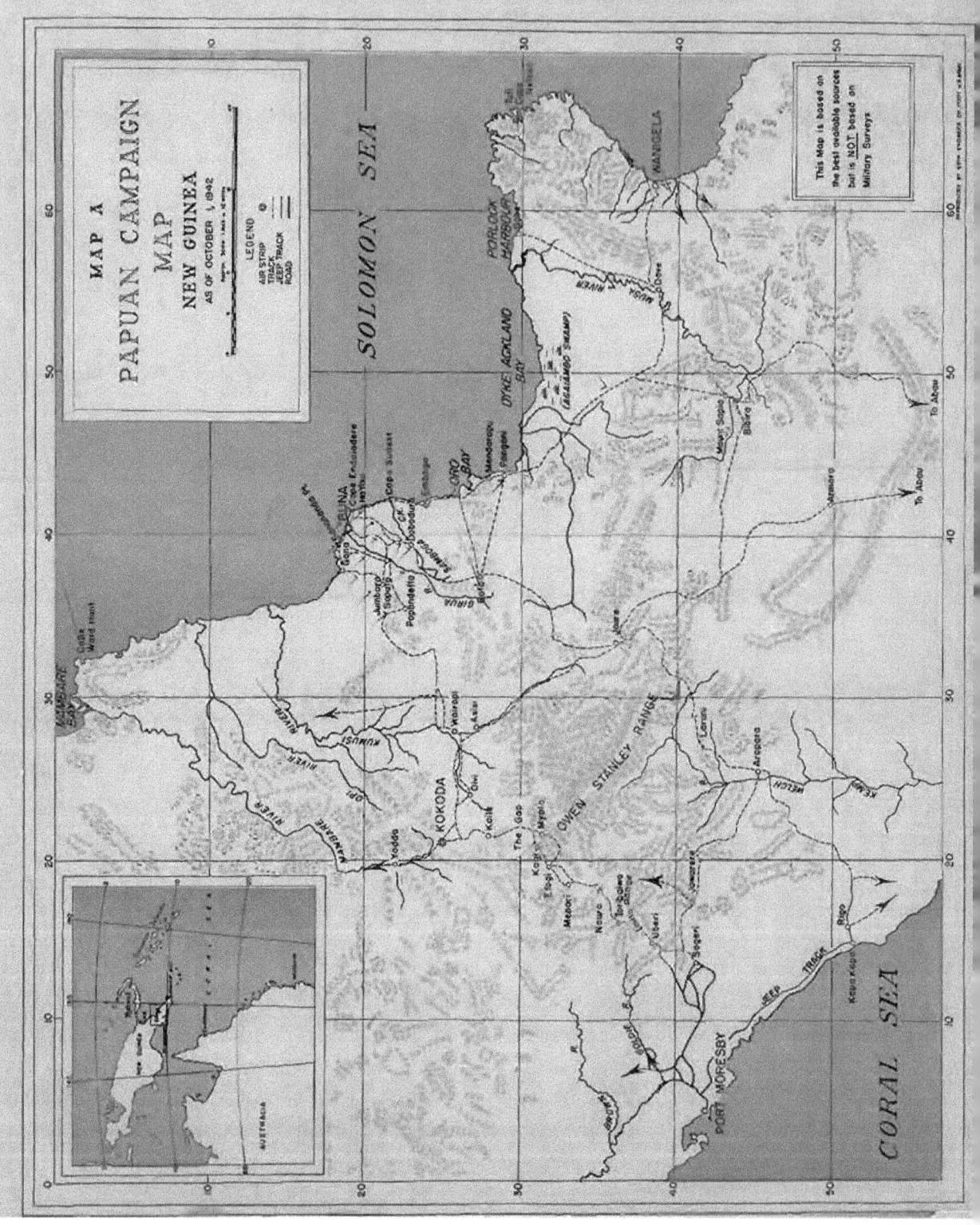

BUNA MISSION
GOV'T. STN.

GIROPA

The Island

Entrance

Creek

Coconut Grove

The Triangle

Government Gardens

To Gerua Gardens

STRIP PT.

OId strip

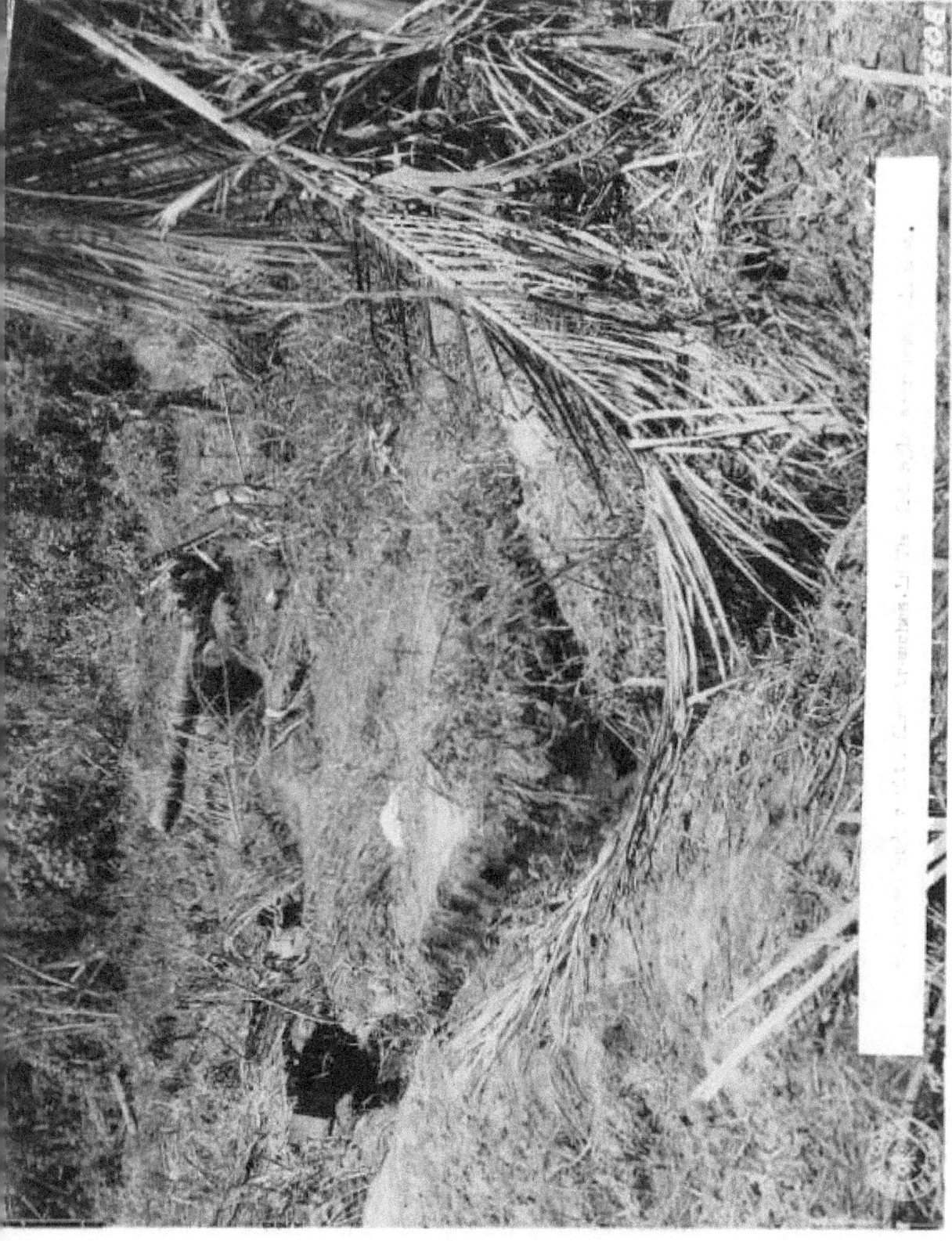

www.ingramcontent.com/pod-product-compliance
Lightning Source LLC
Chambersburg PA
CBHW050501110426
42742CB00018B/3328